BANKEI ZEN

Translations from the Record
of Bankei

Portrait of Bankei, said to be a self-portrait. Property of the
Yaku shi-in, Kawasaki. (*Courtesy Daizō shuppan*)

BANKEI ZEN
Translations from the Record of Bankei

by PETER HASKEL

Yoshito Hakeda, *Editor*
Foreword by Mary Farkas

GROVE PRESS, INC./NEW YORK

*The author wishes to acknowledge the cooperation
of the First Zen Institute of America, New York.*

First Evergreen Edition 1984
First Printing 1984
ISBN: 0-394-62493-9
Library of Congress Catalog Card Number: 83-81372

Library of Congress Cataloging in Publication Data
Bankei, 1622–1693.
  Bankei Zen.
  Translated from the Japanese.
  1. Zen Buddhism—Doctrines—Early works to 1800.
I. Hakeda, Yoshito S. II. Haskel, Peter. III. Title.
BQ9399.E573E5 1984   294.3'927   83-81372
ISBN 0-394-53524-3 (hard)
ISBN 0-394-62493-9 (pbk.)

Manufactured in the United States of America

GROVE PRESS, INC., 196 West Houston Street, New York,
N.Y., 10014

PRE

TO MY TEACHER, YOSHITO HAKEDA, *who spoke directly with the masters of long ago and taught me to listen, this book is gratefully dedicated.*

CONTENTS

Opening of the sermons . . . Listen carefully . . . Precepts . . . The same old thing . . . I don't talk about
Buddhism . . . Meeting masters: Dōsha and Ingen
. . . I'm ready to be your witness! . . . Growing up
deluded . . . Thirty days in the Unborn . . . Ask me
and I'll tell you . . . "The Kappa" . . . Don't beat
sleeping monks . . . Mind reading . . . Moving ahead/
sliding back . . . Old wastepaper . . . Self-centeredness . . . Bankei's Kannon . . . Getting sidetracked
. . . Self-power/other-power . . . Dreams . . . Everybody has the Buddha Mind . . . Being living buddhas
. . . Servants, samurai, husbands and wives . . .
"Buddha" Magoemon . . . Like little children of three
or four . . . Getting angry . . . Blindness and the
Unborn

ILLUSTRATIONS

FOREWORD

These days many people travel hundreds or thousands of miles to see or hear Zen masters. Some meet them. Some study with them. Few have a chance to ask them: What shall I do with my anger, jealousy, hate, fear, sorrow, ambition, delusions—all the problems that occupy human minds? And how shall I deal with my work, my mother and father, my children, my husband or wife, my servants, my employers—the relations that make up human life? Can Zen help me?

If the Zen Master Bankei were available for consultation at a nearby street corner today, he'd be saying much the same things he did to comfort and enlighten the parade of housewives, merchants, soldiers, officials, monks and thieves who sought guidance from him three centuries ago.

Bankei, the enlightened human being, shares his own experience with us as a real person, speaking his own real words. The advice he gives strikes right to the heart. It is highly personal, not theoretical or abstract. The nature of human beings has changed very little through the centuries, despite numerous efforts to change it. Nor does it seem likely to be less full of passion, jealousy and hate in the next thousand years, here or in outer space.

When Bankei had completed his spiritual training and monastic career, which included the founding of a number of temples and the training of innumerable monks and priests, his true concern was with the problems of ordinary people. He had wanted to share what he had discovered with his mother, his first audience, and, I believe, was finally able to do so before she died, a very old lady. He wants us to have it too.

Peter Haskel has found Bankei's real voice. In this fine work by a young translator who has lived intimately with Bankei for the last ten years and knows him through and through, we are brought smack into Bankei's world. It seems to be no translation at all. Although all the tools of scholarship have been meticulously used, no traces of them mar the polish.

No one needs to explain what Bankei means. His seventeenth-century metaphors and logic can be used or discarded without disturbing the substance of his teaching. What comes through is often just good hard common sense. Except for one thing: the Unborn Buddha Mind. Whether called by this name or any other, it is the heart of Zen as well as the core of Bankei's teaching. Bankei's approach shows that there is no need to be Japanese or imitate the Japanese to appreciate or acquire it.

MARY FARKAS
First Zen Institute of America
New York City, April 1983

PREFACE

My first encounter with Bankei was in the fall of 1972. I had arrived at Columbia University two years earlier, hoping to study the history of Japanese Rinzai Zen, but my general coursework and the extreme difficulties of mastering written Japanese had left me time for little else. Now that I was finally to begin my own research, all that remained was to choose a suitable topic. Brimming with confidence and armed with a list of high-sounding proposals, I went to see my advisor, Professor Yoshito Hakeda. He listened patiently, nodded his head, and then, ignoring all my carefully prepared suggestions, asked me if I had considered working on the seventeenth-century Zen master Bankei. My disappointment must have shown. Although I had never actually read Bankei, I had a vague impression of him as a kind of subversive in the world of Zen, a heretical figure who didn't believe in rules, dispensed with koans and tried to popularize and simplify the deadly serious business of enlightenment. I was hoping to deal with a Zen master closer to the "orthodox" tradition, I tried to explain, perhaps one of the great teachers of the Middle Ages. "Take a look at Bankei's sermons if you have a chance," Professor Hakeda urged, "you may find them interesting." My skepticism remained, however, and I did nothing further about Bankei, determined to find a more "respectable" topic of my own choosing.

The following year, Professor Hakeda raised the subject

of Bankei again, and, in spite of my obvious reluctance, pressed on me a small volume of Bankei's sermons. "Try reading a few," he said.

Courtesy required that I at least glance over the text, and late that evening I turned to the first sermon and slowly began to read it through. What I found took me completely by surprise. Bankei's approach to Zen was unlike anything I had ever imagined. Here was a living person addressing an audience of actual men and women, speaking to them in plain language about the most intimate, ordinary and persistent human problems. He answered their questions, listened to their stories, offered the most surprising advice. He told them about his own life as well—the mistakes he'd made, the troubles he'd had, the people whom he'd met. There was something refreshingly original and direct about Bankei's *fushō zen*, his teaching of the "Unborn." "Here it is," Bankei seemed to say, "it really works! I did it, and you can too."

The further I read, the more entranced I became. The next three nights, I could barely sleep. When I returned to Professor Hakeda's office, I told him about my experience. "You see," he said, laughing, "I knew that Bankei was for you!"

On my next visit, I arrived with a partial translation of the first sermon and began to read through the text, with Professor Hakeda making comments and corrections as I proceeded. This was the first of many such meetings which continued for nearly ten years and of which this book is the result. The work is, in a real sense, a tribute to Professor Hakeda. Without his assistance, his unfailing patience, wisdom and encouragement, it would never have come into being.

Among the others who contributed to the present work, Mary Farkas, Director of the First Zen Institute of America, deserves particular mention. She has generously given her time and attention to reviewing the manuscript at every stage, offering countless valuable suggestions. I am also deeply grateful to Professor Philip Yampolsky and the staff of Columbia's East Asian Library for their expert assistance over the years, and to my colleague Ryūichi Abé, who participated in many of the translation sessions. Special thanks are due to Maria Collora, who kindly helped me in editing the English translation, and to Sandy Hackney and John Storm, who read through the completed text. Permission to use photographs included in the illustrations was graciously extended by the Tokyo publishing firms Daizō shuppan and Shunjūsha and by Mrs. Hiroko Akao of Aboshi, Japan. Finally, I would like to express my appreciation to Hannelore Rosset, my editor at Grove, for the extraordinary care she has lavished on the manuscript.

I have tried to offer Western readers a glimpse into Bankei's singular world, using his own words and those of his disciples and descendants. The translations focus particularly on selections from the *Sermons* and the *Hōgo* (Instruction), for, although a certain amount of repetition occurs in these works, they are our most vivid and authentic records of Bankei's teaching. Also included are a series of Bankei's letters, examples of his poetry, and a sampling of materials from various anthologies composed in Chinese after his death. The criteria that guided my selection in each area were purely subjective: I chose those items that seemed to me most interesting and colorful, those that illumined certain aspects of Bankei's character and times or were otherwise simply charming in themselves. Responsibility for any oversight or errors, here and elsewhere in the book, is wholly my own.

The earliest modern collection of Bankei's teachings, the *Bankei zenji goroku* (Tokyo, 1942), edited by D. T. Suzuki in the *Iwanami bunkō* series, has been largely superseded by two more recent editions that serve as the basis for the present translations. These are the *Bankei zenji zenshū* (Daizō shuppan, Tokyo, 1970), edited by the

Japanese scholar Akao Ryūji, and the *Bankei zenji hōgoshū* (Shunjūsha, Tokyo, 1971), edited by Fujimoto Tsuchishige. Fujimoto, a native of Bankei's hometown of Aboshi, devoted a lifetime to collecting and publishing materials related to the Master and his teachings. All modern students of Bankei owe him a great debt.

Shortly before this book was to go to press, Professor Hakeda passed away after a long and courageous bout with cancer. It was his lifelong desire to revive the true teaching of Buddhism in both East and West, and his entire career was a selfless testament to that endeavor. All of us who knew him will miss him sorely and will always treasure his memory.

PETER HASKEL
New York City
September 1983

INTRODUCTION*

Even in his own day, Bankei's Zen struck people as an anomaly, dramatically different from any religious teaching they had known before. At first, this alarmed them because they weren't sure that what he taught was even Buddhism, much less Zen, and there were severe penalties for associating with anyone professing Christianity or other "heretical" beliefs proscribed by the government. By the end of his career, however, Bankei had emerged as something of a celebrity. People trekked from every corner of Japan to hear his talks, and the overflow audiences had to be accommodated in separate shifts. His following embraced nearly every segment of Japanese society: samurai with their families and retainers, merchants, artisans, farmers, servants, even gamblers and gangsters, as well as monks and nuns of all the Buddhist sects, crowded the temples where he spoke. Most came to listen, to learn about Bankei's unusual teaching, but others arrived with special problems, hoping to solicit his advice. Whether it was a monk with trouble meditating, a layman afraid of thunder, a farmer with a bad temper, or a local family feud, Bankei's approach was essentially the same. What-

*My principal source for the Medieval period has been Tamamura Takeji's multi-volume *Nihon zenshūshi ronshū* (Kyoto: Shibunkaku shuppan, 1976–1981), while for the history of Tokugawa Zen, I consulted a variety of primary and secondary sources. The information on Bankei's biography is based mainly on Fujimoto Tsuchishige's *Bankei kokushi no kenkyū* (Tokyo: Shunjūsha, 1971).

ever the problem, for Bankei there was really only one solution: to deal with things on a wholly new basis—to let go, to be natural, to have faith in one's real, "original" mind. He called this his teaching of the Unborn, or the Unborn Buddha Mind. Everyone has this unborn mind, Bankei said; it isn't mysterious or remote, but here and now, functioning, alive, "marvelously illuminating and smoothly managing everything." There's no need to obtain the Buddha Mind since it's been there all along. People only have to abide in it, to use it, to open their eyes. It was easy if they just knew how, and he was there to tell them. That was the message Bankei brought.

In 1622, when Bankei was born, Japan had only recently emerged from a long period of turmoil. Contending warlords had rent the country throughout much of the sixteenth century, and the decisive victory of the Tokugawa forces and their allies in 1600 inaugurated a new and largely peaceful era that was to last over two and one half centuries and leave an indelible mark on much of Japanese life. Though claiming to follow the principles of Confucian ethics, the Tokugawa government was, in effect, a military dictatorship, and its primary concern was to maintain firm control over every area of Japanese society. A rigid class system was instituted, with the samurai, or warrior caste, at the top of the social order, followed by the farmers, craftsmen and merchants who formed the broad mass of the population. Social discipline was strict and enforced at every level through patterns of collective responsibility. Dissent was virtually unknown, and punishment, even for a samurai, could be swift and brutal.

The Buddhist sects too were organized into authoritarian structures, each directly responsible to the government. Although Buddhism was under attack from Confucian officials who viewed the priesthood as parasitic and corrupt, the Tokugawa shoguns themselves remained important patrons, and throughout the Tokugawa period

(1600–1867/1868) the government found the temples invaluable tools in its campaign to root out Christianity, which had been banned as a subversive foreign belief. As proof that they were not "secret Christians," all Japanese families were required to maintain membership in a parish temple, whose priest regularly issued certificates attesting their support. A guaranteed source of income for the temples, the parish system proved a veritable windfall for Buddhism. The power of the parish priest to grant or withhold the required temple certificate, however, offered clear opportunity for abuse, and cases of extortion by unscrupulous clerics were not unknown.

Like the other schools of Buddhism, the Zen sect benefited from the economic security provided by the parish system, but for many Zen monks, the early Tokugawa period was a time of crisis and intense self-examination. Though, materially, many of the temples had prospered during the years of civil war, the teaching of Zen itself had seriously declined. In the course of the fifteenth and sixteenth centuries, Zen study had degenerated into a type of secret oral transmission strongly influenced by Esoteric Buddhism, and the result was a formalized and lifeless affair in which the experience of enlightenment had little or no part. The situation was the same in both the Rinzai and Sōtō sects, the leading schools of Japanese Zen founded during the Middle Ages.

By the beginning of the Tokugawa period, a reaction had set in, and the secret oral transmission was gradually abandoned. Nevertheless, there was no general agreement on the best means to revive Zen in the new age. Different methods were proposed, and a dialogue of sorts continued in both sects throughout the seventeenth century. For many, the answer lay in a return to the past, a restoration of the teachings of the great Medieval founders. The Sōtō school, for example, sought to establish an identity based on the works of its founder Dōgen Kigen (1200–1253), who had been relatively neglected during the late Middle Ages. In the Rinzai school, the center of revival was the Myōshinji, the great headquarters temple in Kyoto with branches throughout Japan. Here, no figures comparable to Dōgen existed, and the retrospective impulse expressed itself in an enthusiasm for the original "koan" Zen that the early teachers of the line had received from Sung China.* This movement in the Myōshinji culminated in the teachings of the eighteenth-century master Hakuin Ekaku (1686–1769) and his disciples, who created the system of koan study still in use in Japanese Rinzai temples. Reverence for the sects' founders was accompanied by a new emphasis on the purity of lines of transmission, the "silent transmission" of enlightenment from mind to mind across the generations that was considered a key feature of the Zen school. The transmission was usually witnessed by the teacher's *inka*, or "seal of approval," his written sanction of the student's enlightenment experience, and these documents were carefully preserved in many Japanese Zen temples. Both schools also witnessed a renewed interest in scholarship, which many felt could offer answers to the dilemmas of the present by providing suitable models from the past.

There were some, however, who believed the problems confronting Zen too deep-rooted to be solved through such reforms, however well-intentioned. For these monks, what was lacking in contemporary Zen was the enlightenment experience itself. With Japanese Zen in decline for the last two hundred years, they argued, no enlightened masters remained to carry on the teaching; it was now up to the individual to enlighten himself and even to sanction his own experience.

Such "independents," men like Suzuki Shōsan (1579–1655), Ungo Kiyō (1582–1659) and Daigu Sōchiku (1584–1669), were primarily self-made masters, colorful individ-

---

*The Sung Dynasty lasted from 960 till 1279.

ualists who owed little to their own teachers. Shōsan came to Zen later in life, taking the tonsure after a successful career as a samurai, but he continued to insist that the warrior's role was better suited to Zen study than the priest's. The only true Buddhism, Shōsan declared, was realized in actual life, in the thick of battle or at work in the fields. He dismissed conventional Zen meditation practices and urged his students to discipline mind and body by imitating the fierce attitude of the Niō, the powerful guardian kings whose images flank the gates of Buddhist temples. Unlike Shōsan, Ungo and Daigu were career priests who had already received their teachers' sanction as Zen masters when they became disillusioned, renounced their previous achievements and set out once again in middle age on the search for enlightenment. Both succeeded, but entirely on their own and only after much hardship and struggle. Ungo's teaching was strongly imbued with pietism, while Daigu's was wildly eccentric; but, like Bankei, both felt that no qualified master existed in Japan to testify to their enlightenment and so were forced to confirm their realization for themselves.

Other Zen monks, while acknowledging that Japanese Zen had grown stagnant, saw promise in the arrival of a new wave of Chinese teachers from the continent. Despite language difficulties—none of the newcomers spoke Japanese, and communication was mainly in writing*—masters like Tao-che Ch'ao-yüan (J: Dōsha Chōgen, d. 1662) and Yin-yüan Lung-ch'i (J: Ingen Ryūki, 1592–1673) quickly attracted a wide following to their temples in the Chinese commercial colony at Nagasaki. Chinese Zen, however, had altered considerably since its introduction to Japan in the twelfth and thirteenth centuries. The Ming dynasty (1368–1644) Zen of the Nagasaki temples con-

---

*The Japanese use Chinese characters in their written language, and most Buddhist monks and educated men of the Tokugawa period had at least some familiarity with written Chinese.

tained many syncretic elements, and it was vigorously opposed by traditionalists, masters such as Gudō Tōshoku (1579–1661) of the Myōshinji, who saw themselves upholding the "pure" Zen of their temples' founders. In the end, only Yin-yüan was successful in establishing his lineage in Japan, where it remains a minor branch of Japanese Zen known as the Ōbaku school,* remembered largely for its influence on painting and calligraphy and famous for its *shōjin ryōri*, or Buddhist vegetarian cuisine.

As even these limited examples make clear, Zen in seventeenth-century Japan was never monolithic, but a series of diverse and at times divergent streams, varied approaches to the problems of how to restore integrity to the teaching after two hundred years of protracted decline. While Bankei's style of Zen was unique, he was distinctly a man of his time and shared many important features with his contemporaries. Even Bankei's originality, his bold self-confidence and iconoclasm were themselves characteristic of certain strains in the Zen world of his day.

Overall, however, Bankei's Zen was essentially a personal development, and at the heart of the teaching of the Unborn lies Bankei's own life story. Bankei himself referred to it frequently in addressing his audiences, urging them not to repeat his mistakes and reminding them how lucky they were to have the benefit of his own hard-won experience.

Bankei was born in 1622 in Hamada, a district of the town of Aboshi,† then a native port on Japan's inland sea. His father was a Confucian, a *rōnin*, or masterless samurai, from the island of Shikoku‡. Through the aid of a

---

*Ōbaku is the Japanese reading of Huang-po, the name of the mountain on which Yin-yüan's Chinese temple stood in what is now Fukien province.
†Today, Aboshi forms part of Himeji City in Hyōgō Prefecture, but in Bankei's day, it belonged to the old province of Harima.
‡One of the four major islands that make up the Japanese archipelago. The others are Kyushu, Hokkaido, and the main island, Honshu.

village headman, Nakabori Sukeyasu, he was adopted into a local family and settled in Hamada, where he became a doctor, a popular occupation among former samurai. Bankei was the third of three sons, and when his father died in 1632, the eldest, Tadayasu, became head of the household. Bankei was always close to his mother, and remained devoted to her throughout his life, but, by all accounts, he and his older brother were temperamental opposites. Like his father, Tadayasu seems to have been a Confucian, a stern moralist with a conviction of the importance of serious study and obedience. By contrast, the young Bankei tended to be wild, unruly and defiant, a ringleader in any mischief and the village champion at rock fighting.

The inevitable confrontation occurred when, at about age eleven, Bankei was sent for lessons at the neighborhood school. Almost from the start he rebelled against the lifeless character of the standard curriculum, which centered on rote memorization of the *Great Learning* (CH: *Ta-hsüeh*), an important Confucian classic. As Bankei tells us in the *Sermons*, his curiosity was aroused by the opening words of the text: "The Way of the Great Learning lies in illuminating the Bright Virtue."

The Bright Virtue (CH: *ming-te*) is one of the key concepts of the Great Learning. It was often interpreted as a kind of dynamic intuitive moral sense that constitutes man's intrinsic nature, and it is likely that Bankei received some such explanation on questioning the local Confucian scholars. But when he pressed them, no one actually seemed to know what the Bright Virtue was, and Bankei was left to puzzle out the problem for himself. Disappointed and consumed by doubts, he eventually began to avoid classes. Tadayasu was outraged at his brother's refusal to continue his studies, and life at home became increasingly unpleasant. Bankei, however, had no intention of returning to the village school, and seeing no way out of his predicament, he reportedly concealed himself in the graveyard of the family temple and attempted suicide by swallowing a mouthful of poisonous spiders. Possibly he had been misled about the spiders' deadliness, for the following day he found himself still very much alive and faced with the same unwelcome prospects at home. Tensions between Bankei and his brother continued to build, and Tadayasu finally expelled the young truant from the household.

The questions aroused by the *Great Learning* continued to obsess Bankei, and after vainly consulting the Confucian scholars, his search led him finally to Buddhism. By age thirteen, Bankei had begun to study with the priest at the family temple, where his middle brother had become a monk, and the following year, his father's old friend Nakabori Sukeyasu came to the rescue and constructed a small retreat for Bankei on the mountain behind the Nakabori family home. Bankei practiced alone here for a time, but, still tormented by doubts, soon resumed the quest for a suitable teacher. After briefly studying Esoteric Buddhism under a priest of the Shingon school, his search brought him to the Myōshinji-line Zen master Umpo Zenshō (1572–1653) of the Zuiōji in nearby Akō. Bankei was now sixteen and still driven by his questions about man's original nature, questions he seems to have lumped collectively under the rubric of the Bright Virtue. Nevertheless, he had apparently decided that only Buddhism effectively confronted the sort of problems that concerned him, and of all the Buddhist sects he had tried, Zen seemed the most promising. Accordingly, in 1638 he received the tonsure from Umpo and became his disciple, with the religious name Bankei Yōtaku.

Virtually nothing is known of Umpo's teaching, and, while always grateful for his kindness, Bankei does not appear to have held a high opinion of Umpo's abilities as a Zen master. In 1641 Bankei left the Zuiōji on a four-year pilgrimage, or *angya*, the period of travel and study that is a traditional part of the Zen monk's training. But his old questions remained, and when he returned to Umpo in 1645, he withdrew to a hut in the nearby village of Nonaka and undertook a regimen of strenuous meditation practice.

For two years Bankei now subjected himself to a series of grueling ordeals in a desperate effort to resolve his doubts once and for all, to uncover the truth about man's intrinsic nature. Driven to the brink of death by hunger and exhaustion, success still eluded him, and in the spring of 1647, Bankei lay in his hut, ill and apparently dying, unable even to swallow the food his servant offered.

One day, feeling something peculiar in his throat, he managed to summon the strength to bring up a dark ball of phlegm, spitting it against the wall. Suddenly the whole weight of his illness dissolved, and he realized the answer to his questions—that he'd had the answer with him all along, the innate mind that manages everything, naturally, effortlessly, just as it is. Summoning his astonished servant, he gulped down several bowls of half-cooked rice and was soon on the way to recovery. Bankei tells us that this was when he first realized the Unborn, but it is uncertain when he actually began to use this term. Possibly it was not until much later in his career, when he had already become a successful teacher. In any case, he rarely mentions the Bright Virtue again.

In 1651, word came of the arrival of the Chinese master Tao-che Ch'ao-yüan at the Sūfukuji, a temple founded by the Chinese merchant community in Nagasaki, and Umpo urged Bankei to pay Tao-che a visit. Tao-che spoke no Japanese, but he sized up Bankei immediately and informed him that his enlightenment, while genuine, was not yet complete. Bankei decided to join Tao-che's assembly, and one evening experienced his second enlightenment while sitting in a darkened corner of the Sūfukuji's meditation hall. Presenting his realization to Tao-che, he demanded: "What about the matter of birth and death?" In reply, Tao-che wrote: "Whose birth and death is this?"

Bankei extended both hands. Tao-che took up his brush again, but this time Bankei snatched it away and hurled it to the ground. The following day, Tao-che publicly announced that Bankei had completed his study of Zen and made him the *tenzo*, or temple cook, a position reserved for advanced students in a Zen monastery.

Bankei stayed with Tao-che for approximately one year, receiving his *inka*. Nevertheless, in retrospect he recognized Tao-che's limitations and lamented that, with no enlightened masters available, Tao-che was the best he could do under the circumstances. In 1652, Bankei returned to Harima, but his first attempts to teach were met with suspicion and hostility, and he spent the next year in retreat in the Yoshino Mountains. In this remote rural district, Bankei was warmly received, and it was probably here that he composed the poem known as the *Song of Original Mind* as a kind of informal instruction for the local people. Umpo was now in failing health, and returning to Akō the following winter, Bankei arrived only in time to attend his teacher's funeral.

In Nagasaki, meanwhile, trouble was brewing. Yin-yüan Lung-ch'i, a well-known Chinese master in Tao-che's teaching line, had arrived in 1654, and his faction was attempting to displace Tao-che at the Sūfukuji. Tao-che preferred to withdraw rather than risk a confrontation that could only prove embarrassing to everyone concerned, and Bankei and several other students set out to find another temple for their beleaguered teacher. Bankei's mission was unsuccessful, but his activities on behalf of Tao-che introduced him to two daimyo, or feudal lords, who subsequently became his patrons and disciples: Matsuura Shigenobu (1622–1703), Lord of Hirado, and Katō Yasuoki (1618–1677), Lord of Iyo. Bankei returned for a time to the Sūfukuji, but relations with Yin-yüan's group continued to deteriorate, and in 1658 Tao-che finally returned to China, bidding a tearful farewell to his Japanese pupils.

Bankei, however, was now to become a Zen master in his own right. At Umpo's dying request, his heir Bokuō Sogyū (d. 1694) conferred *inka* on Bankei, who had not been present when Umpo died. This was a common procedure in Japanese Zen temples, and though, technically, it established Bankei as Bokuō's heir, was simply a convenient device to recognize Bankei as Umpo's descendant and to include him in the Shōtaku-ha, Umpo's branch of the Myōshinji teaching line. In 1659, in recognition of his new status, Bankei received advanced rank in the Myōshinji. Still something of the *enfant terrible*, he reportedly elicited objections from traditionalists for refusing to observe the conventions of the ceremony, which included the taking up of koans.

Back in Hamada, too, things were changing for Bankei. He had long ago made peace with Tadayasu, who died in 1661, and in the same year a childhood friend from the village school, Sasaki Nobutsugu (1625–1686), joined his brothers in establishing a temple for Bankei in Hamada, the Ryōmonji, or Dragon Gate Temple. Originally *rōnin*, like Bankei's family, the Sasakis had settled in Hamada and become wealthy merchants, shipowners whose shop name Nadaya was famous throughout Japan. Together with their wives and children, the Sasaki brothers were among Bankei's most loyal supporters and remained the Ryōmonji's principal patrons. The Ryōmonji was only the first of many important temples Bankei received. As his fame spread, he acquired numerous followers among the upper ranks of the samurai—daimyo and their families, who vied for his visits and offered temples in their domains and in the capitals of Kyoto and Edo. *

The following years found Bankei frequently in seclusion at one or another of the cloisters provided by his benefactors, practicing alone, instructing a select group of

---

*The old name for Tokyo.

disciples, or nursing his recurrent illness. Bankei's early struggles had taken a severe toll on his health, and in later life he was often in extreme discomfort, afflicted with chronic stomach spasms and fits of coughing that required intervals of quiet convalescence. Possibly, too, the retreats of the 1660s and '70s were opportunities for Bankei to continue the search for an appropriate method of instruction that led to his mature teaching of the Unborn. But on this our materials from the period are too scanty to permit anything more than speculation.

In any case, the year 1679 marked a significant change in Bankei's approach, with the emphasis shifting to collective practice and public sermons at large *kessei*, the traditional three-month periods of intensive meditation held at Zen temples in the winter and summer. From this time until his death, Bankei continued to conduct important training periods nearly every year, traveling to his various temples and sometimes delivering as many as three talks a day.

Unfortunately, we know little of the actual details of practice at these *kessei* or at Bankei's temples generally. In certain respects, at least, life in Bankei's assemblies was apparently different from that in other teachers' establishments. Bankei, for example, would not tolerate repressive behavior such as the beating or scolding that still characterizes training at many Zen temples; nor would he allow begging by his monks, though the practice was standard in Buddhist monasteries and entirely legal. Nevertheless, in common with most Zen monks, Bankei's students observed daily periods of meditation and chanting, and Bankei himself, like other Japanese Zen teachers of the day, received students in private interviews, performed funeral and memorial services for his patrons and scrupulously upheld the Buddhist precepts in his personal life. All in all, what distinguished Bankei's assemblies from those elsewhere seems to have been more a matter of atmosphere than one of procedure.

Bankei's later years were marked by constant travel between his various temples and patrons. In 1680, he suffered a severe loss with the death of his mother, who had become a Buddhist nun and retired to a convent not far from the Ryōmonji. Bankei had always been fiercely devoted to his mother and insisted that what had originally driven him to realize enlightenment had been, above all, his desire to communicate the truth to her.

In 1690, Bankei was at the height of his career. His teaching of the Unborn had won a vast and devoted following, and in addition to the numerous honors he had received at the Myōshinji, the Emperor now awarded him the personal title *Butchi Kōsai zenji,* "Zen Master of Beneficent Enlightened Wisdom." In the fall, Bankei was invited to deliver a series of public lectures at the Hōshinji in Marugame, the castle town of his daimyo patron Kyōgoku Takatoyo (1655–1694), Lord of Sanuki. Later that year, he conducted the most famous of his training periods, a vast *kessei* at the Ryōmonji, attended by nearly seventeen hundred monks of every sect, some traveling from as far as the Ryukyu Islands. Available space in the Ryōmonji's *zendō,* or meditation hall, was quickly exhausted, and temporary *zendō* had to be improvised to accommodate the flood of new arrivals. The *kessei* was funded and provisioned by the Sasaki brothers, but the crowd of monks grew so immense that the Sasakis panicked and vainly begged Bankei to turn away any further applicants. Despite these setbacks, the *kessei* proved a success and was marred only by the tragic death of Bankei's close disciple Sōen. During the *kessei,* Bankei delivered a total of sixty lectures, many of which were recorded by members of the audience, and these, together with the lectures recorded at Marugame earlier in the year, constitute the bulk of Bankei's surviving sermons.

By 1693, Bankei's health had worsened, and, realizing that little time remained, the Ryōmonji's parishioners hastened to erect a pagoda for him, contributing their own labor to the project. Ordinary men and women, even grandfathers and nursing mothers, arrived to join in the effort, and at night, when their official duties were over, samurai would come to carry on the work by moonlight. That June, returning to the Ryōmonji from a visit to Edo, Bankei became seriously ill. He managed to deliver a final three days of lectures, but his condition continued to worsen, and before the end of September he was dead. His ashes were divided chiefly between the Ryōmonji and his other principal temple, the Nyohōji, erected in Iyo by Lord Katō. In 1740, Bankei was awarded the posthumous Imperial title of *Kokushi*, or "National Master," an honor accorded only six other teachers in the Myōshinji's history.

What was it that made Bankei's teaching of the Unborn so popular in his time? Above all, perhaps, was the fact that the basics of Bankei's Zen were clear and relatively simple. You didn't have to be learned, live in a monastery or even necessarily consider yourself a Buddhist to practice them effectively. Nor did you have to engage in long and arduous discipline. True, Bankei himself had undergone terrible hardships before he realized the Unborn; but only, as he constantly reminded his listeners, because he never met a teacher able to tell him what he had to know. In fact, one could readily attain the Unborn in the comfort of one's own home. It wasn't necessary, or even advisable, Bankei insisted, to follow his own example.

Bankei's entire teaching can be reduced to the single admonition "Abide in the Unborn!" This was Bankei's constant refrain. The term "Unborn" itself is a common one in classical Buddhism, where it generally signifies that which is intrinsic, original, uncreated. Bankei, however, was the first to use this term as the crux of his teaching. Rather than obtaining or practicing the Unborn, he says, one should simply abide in it, because the Unborn is not a state that has to be created, but is already there, perfect and complete, the mind just as it is. There isn't any special method for realizing the Unborn other than to be yourself, to be totally natural and spontaneous in everything you do. This means "letting thoughts arise or cease just as they will," and doing the same in regard to physical sensations, as Bankei indicates in his advice on illness (pp. 61–63) and in his instructions on the art of the lance (pp. 138–39).

The mind, as Bankei describes it, is a dynamic mechanism, reflecting, recording and recalling our impressions of the world, a kind of living mirror that is always in motion, never the same from one instant to the next. Within this mirror mind, thoughts and feelings come and go, appearing, vanishing and reappearing in response to circumstances, neither good nor bad in themselves. Unlike the man of the Unborn, however, the impulsive person suffers from attachment. He is never natural because he is a *slave* to his responses, which he fails to realize are only passing reflections. As a result, he is continually "hung up," entangled in particular thoughts and sensations, obstructing the free flow of the mind. Everything will operate smoothly, Bankei insists, if we only step aside and let it do so. He illustrates this to the members of his audience by pointing out that, even while engrossed in listening to his talk, they automatically register and identify everything else around them—the calls of crows and sparrows, the various colors and aromas, the different sorts of people in the room. No one is deliberately trying to *do* this; it simply happens. That, Bankei says, is how the Unborn functions.

For Bankei, the important thing is letting go, breaking the mold of our self-centeredness (*mi no hiiki*) and bad habits (*kiguse*). These are familiar Japanese terms that Bankei used to describe the chief components of delusion. Self-centeredness is the basis of the false self. It is "ego" in the pejorative sense, the reflex that leads us to judge everything from a narrowly selfish viewpoint. What fuels and informs this attitude is bad habits, character flaws that, like self-centeredness, are the result of conditioning. We grow up imitating the people around us, Bankei says, and in the process acquire certain failings which finally become so ingrained that we mistake them for our real selves. Unlike the Unborn Buddha Mind, however, neither bad habits nor self-centeredness is innate; both are assimilated from outside after birth. When we become deluded, we temporarily forfeit the Buddha Mind we started out with, exchanging it for these learned responses. The moment this occurs, duality intervenes and we leave the original oneness of the Unborn to be "born" into particular states of being—as hungry ghosts, fighting demons, beasts or hell-dwellers—passing fitfully from one to the next, trapped in incessant transmigration. The only way out of this dilemma, Bankei maintains, is to go back the way we came, to return to the unconditioned, the uncreated, the unborn.

"What we have from our parents innately is the Unborn Buddha Mind and nothing else"; "The Buddha Mind is unborn and marvelously illuminating, and with the Unborn everything is perfectly managed"; "Abide in the Unborn Buddha Mind!" These are the basics of Bankei's Zen, his catechism of the Unborn. He explained them over and over in different ways, because he believed the truth of the Unborn was so simple, so straightforward, that anyone could grasp it. In this sense, Bankei's Zen was truly popular. Other Japanese masters had taught lay audiences. But, in most cases, Zen as such was considered far too difficult for ordinary people, and Zen masters' popular teachings, especially those directed to women, scarcely touched on Zen at all. Instead, teachers spoke in general terms, urging the merits of pious activity and discussing concepts from the Buddhist scriptures. Study of the "inner teachings" was generally confined to qualified monks and members of the upper classes and intelligentsia who could follow to some extent the difficult Chinese of the imported Zen texts.

Bankei's position was just the reverse. He maintained that the essence of Zen itself was perfectly plain and direct, and that any person with an open mind could be made to understand. You didn't need to be widely educated or adept at classical Chinese. That sort of thing only got in the way. In fact, the Unborn could best be explained using simple, everyday language. Any other approach was just deceptive. To teach Zen, Bankei insisted, one had to go right to the core, to divest oneself of everything extraneous—all the gimmicks, the technical jargon, the exotic foreign usages.

This was Bankei's principal objection to the koan. Though its origins are obscure, koan Zen was largely a development of the Sung dynasty, when it became popular for Chinese masters to assign their students particular *kung-an* (read as *kōan* in Japanese) or "public cases," named for the model cases that served as guidelines in the Chinese courts of law. The Zen koans were brief and often paradoxical episodes drawn principally from the records of the earlier masters, especially those of the "golden age" of Zen in the T'ang (618–906) and Five Dynasties (907–960) periods.

> A monk asked Yun-men (862/4–949): "What is the Buddha?"
> Yun-men said: "A shit-wiping stick."
>   (*Wu-men kuan*, no. 21)

> A monk asked Chao-chou (778–897): "Why did the Patriarch come from the West?" (That is, what is the ultimate truth that Bodhidharma, the First Patriarch and semi-legendary founder of Chinese Zen, brought from India?)
>   Chao-chou said: "The cypress tree in the garden."
>   (*Wu-men kuan*, no. 37)

Under the teacher's guidance, the student would strive to penetrate the problem presented by his case, generating a "great ball of doubt" as he puzzled over the koan, attempting to break through to enlightenment. Certain teachers compiled popular collections of koans that included responses to each case in the form of poems, comments and substitute answers. The most famous of these were the twelfth-century *Blue Cliff Record* (CH: *Pi-yen lu*, J: *Hekigan roku*) and the thirteenth-century *Gateless Gate* (CH: *Wu-men kuan*, J: *Mumonkan*).

Introduced from China in the twelfth and thirteenth centuries, koan study became a standard form of Zen practice in Japan. However, due in part to the prestige of continental culture, the koan collections with their associated poems and comments were preserved in the original Chinese. The problem was compounded by the language of the koan records themselves, which contained many obscure colloquial expressions, difficult phrases and specialized terms. Japanese students were expected not only to master these but to insert them in the rapid give-and-take of *mondō*, or Zen dialogues, and in their private interviews with the teacher.

Inevitably, this created certain difficulties. The emphasis on such arcane foreign-language material was a serious impediment to practitioners of merely average intellectual ability and threatened to drain much of the spontaneity from the encounter between master and student. Yet, despite its drawbacks, the koan enjoyed enormous popularity in Japanese Zen, and remained an important feature in both the Rinzai and Sōtō sects. The very difficulty of negotiating the koan collections, the technical expertise required to decipher the original texts, made the Zen priesthood a kind of exclusive fraternity that included many specialists in literary Chinese.

The nature of Bankei's own experience of koan study is uncertain. It seems likely that he had some contact with koan Zen in his student days, and evidence indicates that he occasionally used koans for his own disciples. Judging by Bankei's statements in the *Sermons,* however, he abandoned koans altogether in his later years. As Bankei saw it, the whole approach of koan Zen was hopelessly contrived. He rejected the need for familiarity with classical Chinese as an unnecessary encumbrance, and rejected the koan itself as an artificial technique. The original koans, he argued, were not "models," but actual living events. The old masters had simply responded to particular situations that confronted them, naturally accommodating themselves to the needs of the students involved. That was the business of any Zen teacher, to meet each situation on its own terms. There was no need to make people study the words of ancient Chinese monks when you could simply have them look at their *own* "cases," the way in which the Unborn was at work here and now in the actual circumstances of their lives. This was what Bankei called his "direct" teaching, as opposed to koan practice, which he referred to disparagingly as "studying old waste paper." The koan, said Bankei, was merely a device, and teachers who relied on it, or on any other technique, were practicing "devices Zen." Why rely on a device, he argued, when you could have the thing itself?

In this sense, Bankei was a traditionalist. He harked back to the Zen masters of the "golden age" before the triumph of the koan, masters like Lin-chi I-hsüan (J: Rinzai Gigen, d. 860), founder of the Rinzai school. Bankei insisted that his own teachings were the same as Lin-chi's, and the many similarities between the *Sermons* and the *Lin-chi lu* (J: *Rinzai roku*), the record of Lin-chi's teachings, suggest that the Chinese master may have been an important influence on Bankei's Zen.

Taken as a whole, however, Bankei's teaching remains uniquely his own. Ironically, its failure to survive was probably due to the very qualities that made it so distinctive and so attractive to Bankei's students: its close identification with Bankei's own personality and its refusal to associate itself with particular procedures or techniques. Ultimately, "Hakuin Zen," which revived and systematized koan study in Japan, swept the monasteries of the Rinzai school, even infiltrating the Ryōmonji and the other temples of Bankei's line. To Hakuin, Bankei's freewheeling teaching of the Unborn was anathema, and he denounced it emphatically. But the twentieth century has seen renewed interest in Bankei's Zen. The noted Buddhist scholar D. T. Suzuki (1886–1975) became the leading modern champion of Bankei's teaching, hailing it as a refreshing antidote to the strictures of the koan method and ranking Bankei with Dōgen and Hakuin as one of Japan's three great Zen masters. Suzuki and other Japanese scholars began to compile and edit the records of Bankei's teaching, many of which had lain forgotten in various provincial temples, and today Bankei is gaining popularity once again.

Bankei's continued appeal is easy to understand. Though his world was very different from our own, there is something contemporary in much of what he has to say. His sense of freedom, his humanity, his intimate approach to the ultimate problems in terms of people's daily lives seem wholly attuned to the spirit of the present day. And when we turn to the pages of the sermons, Bankei is still there, still curiously alive and "marvelously illuminating."

SERMONS

of the Zen Master
BANKEI

PART I

Opening of the Sermons

When the Zen Master Bankei Butchi Kōsai,[1] founder of the Ryōmonji[2] at Aboshi in Banshū, was at the Great Training Period[3] [held] at the Ryōmonji in the winter of the third year of Genroku,[4] there were 1,683 monks listed in the temple register.[5] Those who attended included not only Sōtō and Rinzai[6] followers but members of the Ritsu, Shingon, Tendai, Pure Land, True Pure Land and Nichiren Schools,[7] with laymen and monks mingled together, thronging round the lecture seat.[8] One sensed the Master was truly the Teacher of Men and Devas[9] for the present age.

At that time, the Master mounted the lecture seat and addressed the assembly of monks and laymen, saying: "We've got a big crowd of both monks and laymen here at this meeting, and I thought I'd tell you about how, when I was young, I struck on the realization that the mind is unborn. This part about 'the mind,' [though,] is something secondary. You monks, when you abide only in the Unborn, [will find that] in the Unborn, there's nothing anyone needs to tell you, nothing you need to hear. Because the Buddha Mind is unborn and marvelously illuminating, it gets easily turned into whatever comes along. So, as long as I'm telling the lay people here not to change themselves into these different things that come their way and trade their

Buddha Mind for thoughts, you monks may as well listen too!"

Listen carefully

The Master addressed the assembly: "Among all you people here today there's not a single one who's an unenlightened being. Everyone here is a buddha. So listen carefully! What you all have from your parents innately is the Unborn Buddha Mind alone. There's nothing else you have innately. This Buddha Mind you have from your parents innately is truly unborn and marvelously illuminating. That which is unborn is the Buddha Mind; the Buddha Mind is unborn and marvelously illuminating, and, what's more, with this Unborn, everything is perfectly managed. The actual proof of this Unborn which perfectly manages [everything] is that, as you're all turned this way listening to me talk, if out back there's the cawing of crows, the chirping of sparrows or the rustling of the wind, even though you're not deliberately trying to hear each of these sounds, you recognize and distinguish each one. The voices of the crows and sparrows, the rustling of the wind—you hear them without making any mistake about them, and that's what's called hearing with the Unborn. In this way, all things are perfectly managed with the Unborn. This is the actual proof of the Unborn. Conclusively realize that what's unborn and marvelously illuminating is truly the Buddha Mind, straightaway abiding in the Unborn Buddha Mind just as it is, and you're a living tathagata[10] from today forever after. Since, when you realize conclusively, you abide like this in the Buddha Mind from today on, my school is called the School of Buddha Mind.[11]

"Well, then, while you're all turned this way listening to me talk, you don't mistake the chirp of a sparrow out back for the caw of a crow, the sound of a gong for that of a drum, a man's voice for a woman's, an adult's voice for a child's—you clearly recognize and distinguish each sound you hear without making any mistake. That's the marvelously illuminating dynamic function. It's none other than the Buddha Mind, unborn and marvelously illuminating, the actual proof of the marvelously illuminating [nature of the Buddha Mind].

"I doubt there's anyone among the people here now who'd say: 'I heard [what I did] because I was deliberately *trying* to hear it.' If anyone says he did, he's a liar. Wondering, 'What's Bankei telling us?' all of you are turned this way, intent only on hearing what I'm saying; no one's deliberately trying to hear the various sounds coming from out back. That's why, when all of a sudden these sounds appear and you recognize and distinguish them, hearing them without any mistake, you're hearing with the Unborn Buddha Mind. Nobody here can claim he heard these sounds because he'd made up his mind beforehand to listen for them when they were made. So, in fact, you're listening with the Unborn.

"Everyone who conclusively realizes that what is unborn and marvelously illuminating is truly the Buddha Mind, abiding in the Unborn Buddha Mind, is a living tathagata from today forever after. Even 'buddha' is just a name given to traces that have arisen,[12] so, from the standpoint of the Unborn, it's only a secondary matter, a peripheral concern. The man of the Unborn abides at the *source* of all buddhas. That which is unborn is the source of all things, the starting point of all things. There's nothing more original than the Unborn, nothing prior to it. That's why, when you abide in the Unborn, you abide at the source of all buddhas; so it's something wonderfully precious. There's no question of 'perishing' here, so when you abide in the Unborn, it's superfluous to speak about the Imperishable[13] too. That's the reason I only talk about the Unborn and don't mention the Imperishable. What isn't created can't be destroyed, so since it's unborn, it's obvious it's imperishable without having to mention it. Isn't that so?

"Of course, the expression 'unborn and imperishable'[14] has appeared here and there in the sutras and records from times of old—but not the actual *proof* of the Unborn. Everyone just learns the expression 'unborn and imperishable' and goes about repeating it; but when it comes to realizing conclusively and actually getting right to the heart of the matter, they haven't any idea of what the Unborn is.

"When I was twenty-six, I first hit on the realization that all things are perfectly managed with the Unborn, and, in the forty years since, I've taught everyone with the actual proof of the Unborn: that what you have from your parents innately is the Unborn Buddha Mind—the Buddha Mind which is truly unborn and marvelously illuminating. I was the first to teach this. I'm sure that even among you monks in the assembly now, and everyone else too, nobody's heard of anyone before me who taught people with the actual proof of the Unborn—that the Buddha Mind is truly Unborn and marvelously illuminating. I was the first to teach this. If anyone claims he's heard of somebody before me who taught people with the actual proof of the Unborn, he's a liar!

"When you abide in the Unborn, you're abiding at the source of all things. What the buddhas of the past realized was the Unborn Buddha Mind; and what buddhas in the future will realize is the Unborn Buddha Mind too. We today are living in the Degenerate Age of Buddhism,[15] yet when there's even one man who abides in the Unborn, the true teaching[16] has been restored to the world. All of you, isn't it so? It certainly is! When you've conclusively realized this, then and there you'll open the eye that sees into men's minds, and that's why my school is called the Clear-Eyed School.[17] When the eye that sees into men is manifested, *whenever* it happens to be,[18] that moment is the complete realization of the Dharma.[19] I want you to know this. Whoever you may be, at that moment, you are my heir!"

Precepts

A certain master of the Precepts School[20] asked: "Doesn't your Reverence observe the precepts?"

The Master said: "Originally, what people call the precepts were all for wicked monks who broke the rules; for the man who abides in the Unborn Buddha Mind, there's no need for precepts. The precepts were taught to help sentient beings—they weren't taught to help buddhas! What everyone has from his parents innately is the Unborn Buddha Mind alone, so abide in the Unborn Buddha Mind. When you abide in the Unborn Buddha Mind, you're a living buddha here today, and that living buddha certainly isn't going to concoct anything like taking the precepts, so there aren't any precepts for him to take. To concoct anything like taking the precepts is not what's meant by the Unborn Buddha Mind. When you abide in the Unborn Buddha Mind, there's no way you can violate the precepts. From the standpoint of the Unborn, the precepts too are secondary, peripheral concerns; in the place of the Unborn, there's really no such thing as precepts. . . ."

The same old thing

"A certain teacher of Buddhism told me: 'Instead of teaching the same old thing in your sermons day after day, you ought to throw in a few Buddhist miracle stories[21] once in a while and give people a refreshing change of pace.' Of course, he could be right. I may be thickheaded, but provided something is really helpful to people, then, thickheaded or not, I'm not beyond memorizing one or two old stories if I put my mind to it. However, teaching this sort of thing is like feeding poison to sentient beings. And feeding people poison is something I certainly can't do!"

I don't talk about Buddhism

The Master further said: "I don't teach people by quoting from the words of the buddhas and patriarchs.[22] Since I can manage simply by dealing with people's own selves, there's no need on top of that to quote the words of the buddhas and patriarchs too. I don't talk about Buddhism, and I don't talk about Zen. There's really no need to talk about these things. Since I can manage perfectly just by dealing with people's own selves as they are right here today, there's no need for me to talk about Buddhism, or Zen either. . . ."

*   *   *

Meeting masters: Dōsha and Ingen

"Until the age of thirty, I continued to wear my *jittoku*[23] robes without putting on a proper monk's robe. When I was thirty, however, my teacher[24] suggested I go to meet the Chinese Zen Master Dōsha Chōgen of Naninsan,[25] who'd recently landed at Nagasaki. I decided to go, and my teacher told me: 'Up to now you've been able to get by with your *jittoku* robes; but now that you're going to call on a real Chinese monk, they won't do. As it's also for the sake of the Dharma, from here on you'd better wear a proper monk's robe, so go put one on and call on Dōsha.'

"And that's how, at the age of thirty, following my teacher's advice, I put on a monk's robe for the first time and went off to see Dōsha. I immediately presented my understanding. Dōsha sized me up at a glance and told me: 'You have transcended birth and death!'

"Among the Zen teachers at that time, only Dōsha was able, to this modest extent, to confirm for me my experience of enlightenment; but, even so, I wasn't fully satisfied. Now, looking back, today I wouldn't even find Dōsha acceptable. If only Dōsha had gone on living till now, I might have made a better man of him. But he was an unlucky fellow and died young, to my great regret."

"When I was a member of Dōsha's assembly, an invitation was sent to China to [the Zen Master] Ingen.[26] I was among those who consulted on this, and, fortunately, Ingen arrived in Japan while I was with Dōsha, landing at the harbor in Nagasaki.[27] I went along to welcome him, but the moment Ingen stepped ashore from the boat, I realized he wasn't a man of the Unborn, and that's why I never studied with him."

I'm ready to be your witness!

"All of you right now are extremely fortunate. When I was young, either there were no enlightened teachers about, or else, if there were, I just wasn't lucky enough to meet them, and being from youth exceedingly thickheaded, I suffered unimaginable hardships. How uselessly I struggled! I can't forget those wasted efforts, which have left a deep impression on me. I had to learn the hard way, from experience. That's why, in my desire to have all of you attain complete realization of the Dharma in perfect comfort, at your ease, and *without* any useless struggle, I do my best to come out like this every day and urge you on. All of you should consider yourselves fortunate. Where could you ever find this sort of opportunity!

"Although I didn't intend to tell you about this—how when I was young I struggled uselessly thanks to my own thickheadedness—if among the young people here there's anyone who struggles as I did, thinking it's impossible to attain complete realization of the Dharma without doing so, why then I'll be to blame. So, although I didn't intend to tell you, you young people listen carefully! Since, without struggling as I did, you can attain complete realization of the Dharma, first of all let me tell you about my own struggles, and that way you'll realize that you can attain complete realization without going and doing as Bankei did. While you listen, I want you to keep this in mind. Well, then, I'll begin, so pay close attention!

"My father, whose original family name was Suga,²⁸ was a *rōnin*²⁹ from Shikoku³⁰ and a Confucian. He came and settled in this area,³¹ where I was born, but died while I was still a small child, leaving my mother to raise me. I was, according to her story, a naughty boy, and as leader of all the children in the neighborhood would get into mischief. However, my mother told me that from the time I was two or three I'd already developed a horror of death: when I cried, if someone made believe he were dying, or if I was told about someone's having died, I'd instantly dry my tears and even give up any mischief I happened to be engaged in.

"Gradually I grew up. At the time I was young, Confucianism was very popular hereabouts, and my mother sent me to a teacher to learn to read the *Great Learning* aloud by rote.³² But when I came to the passage that states, 'The Way of the Great Learning lies in illuminating the Bright Virtue,'³³ I couldn't make out what this Bright Virtue was, and, beset by doubt, puzzled over it for some time.

"At one point, I went and questioned some Confucian scholars. 'What sort of thing *is* this Bright Virtue?' I asked them, 'Just what is the Bright Virtue, anyway?' But there wasn't one of them who knew.

"However, one of the Confucian scholars told me: 'Difficult matters like this are the kind of things Zen monks understand, so go and ask a Zen monk. Even though with our mouths we can talk endlessly about the meaning of the words and letters in the Classics,[34] when it comes to just what sort of thing the Bright Virtue *is*, we really have no idea.'

" 'Well,' I thought, finding myself still in the dark, 'so that's how things are!' But since there were no Zen monks hereabouts then, I had no chance to ask anyone. Nevertheless, then and there I resolved that somehow I'd realize the meaning of this Bright Virtue and tell my aged mother about it before she died. Even before realizing it myself, I wanted above all to communicate it to my mother who, being old, might die at any time. Hoping to resolve this matter of the Bright Virtue, I floundered about desperately, scurrying all over. A talk here, a lecture there—whenever I learned there was a sermon, no matter where it was, I hurried right off to hear it. Returning home, I reported to my mother anything significant I might have heard, but my question about the Bright Virtue was still unresolved.

"Next, I made up my mind to visit a master of this Zen school. When I asked him about the Bright Virtue, he told me: 'If you want to understand the Bright Virtue, do zazen[35] and the Bright Virtue will be understood.'

"As a result, after this I immediately took up the practice of zazen. Here, I'd go into the mountains, eating nothing for seven or even ten whole days; there, I'd find some cliffs, and, seated on a pointed rock, pull up my robes, with my bare backside right against the stone, determined to meditate to the very end, even if it killed me, and refusing to leave my seat until I simply tumbled down. Since there was no way I could even ask anyone to bring me food, I often didn't eat for days. But all I cared about was resolving the Bright Virtue, so I didn't mind that I was faint from hunger, and refused to let it bother me. Despite it all, though, I still couldn't settle my question about the Bright Virtue.

"After this, I returned to my native area, built a small hut for myself and went into retreat. At times, totally absorbed in practicing the *nembutsu*,[36] I wouldn't lie down, night or day.

"So I floundered about desperately, trying in every way, but my question about the Bright Virtue was still unresolved. Without much care for my life, I'd driven my whole body so mercilessly that the skin on my backside had become torn, with the result that I could only sit with the most painful difficulty. However, as I look back on it now, in those years I was still in fine fettle, and, in spite of everything, wouldn't lie down to rest for even a day. All the same, since I was suffering from the torn flesh on my backside, I had to sit on bundles of Sugihara[37] paper that I'd spread under me and replace one after another. Despite this precaution, blood issued constantly from my backside, and with the pain, it became difficult to sit, so that I sometimes had to spread wads of cotton and whatnot underneath me. Even with all that, I could pass an entire day and night without ever lying down.

"The strain of those years finally caught up with me, and I became gravely ill. Without having settled my question about the Bright Virtue, I'd struggled with it tirelessly for a long time, enduring bitter hardship. My illness gradually worsened now, my body grew weak, and when I'd bring up phlegm, there'd emerge thumb-size gobs of bloody sputum that rolled along congealing into balls. Sometimes when I'd spit against the wall, the sputum was so heavy it rolled right down. At this time, everyone concerned about me said: 'This simply won't do! You've got to rest and nurse yourself back to health.' So, following their advice, I retired to my hut, taking on a manservant.

"But gradually my illness reached a critical point, and for a full seven days I was unable to swallow any food and could get nothing down apart from some thin rice gruel. Because of this, I realized I was on the verge of death. 'Ah, well,' I said to myself, 'there's nothing to be done.' But really I had no particular regret other than the thought that I was going to die without realizing my long-cherished desire.

"Just then, I had a strange sensation in my throat, and when I spit against the wall, I noticed the sputum had congealed into a jet-black lump like a soapberry,[38] rolling down the surface. After that, the inside of my chest felt curiously refreshed, and that's when it suddenly struck me: 'Everything is perfectly managed with the Unborn, and because up till today I couldn't see this, I've just been uselessly knocking myself out!' Finally I saw the mistake I'd been making!

"My spirit now felt clear and buoyant, my appetite returned, and I called to my servant: 'I want to eat some rice gruel. Go and prepare it!' My servant, meanwhile, thought this a strange request indeed for a man who until then had been on the very brink of death. 'Thank heavens!' he exclaimed, delighted, and hurried right off in confusion to prepare the gruel. In his hurry to feed me something, he promptly served the rice gruel, but what he fed me hadn't all been fully cooked. I didn't even care, and went right ahead and devoured two or three bowlsful without any ill effects. After that, I gradually got well again and have lived to this day.[39] So I realized my cherished desire after all, and explained things to my mother too before she passed away.[40]

"Ever since I realized that everything is perfectly managed with the Unborn, there hasn't been a person in the land who could refute me. If only, when I was desperately floundering, there had been some man of realization who could have just told me right at the start, the way I'm doing now for you, I might have been spared my useless struggles; but there wasn't any such person to be found, and with no one to tell me, I struggled long and hard, driving myself beyond all endurance. That's why, even today, I'm still a sick man and can't come out to meet with you as much as I would like.

"At all events, once I realized the fact that everything is perfectly managed with the Unborn, I wanted to try to talk this over with someone. And while I was wondering whom to meet and discuss this with, my teacher[41] told me: 'In Mino,[42] there's a teacher named Gudō,[43] who's said to be a good man. He may be able to confirm your experience, so you'd better go try to speak with him.'

"Hoping to meet Gudō and speak with him, I followed my teacher's instructions and set out to visit him in Mino, only to find that he wasn't at home, being just then in Edo.[44] So, as it turned out, we never met, and I hadn't any chance to talk with him.

"Having come all this way and not spoken to anyone, I decided that, rather than just going back with nothing accomplished, I'd visit the Zen teachers in the area.

" 'I'm a Zen monk from Banshū,'[45] I said when I met them, 'and I've come here solely in hope of meeting you and receiving your teaching.'

"When the teachers had presented *their* instruction, I took the liberty of putting in a word myself. 'I realize it's impertinent of me,' I told them, 'but please excuse me when I say that, while I'm not ungrateful for the instruction you've given, I get a feeling as if someone were trying to scratch an itchy spot through my shoe. Unless you reach right in and scratch, you won't get to my real bones and marrow,[46] and things won't be settled through and through.'

"Like the honest teachers they were, they told me: 'Yes, it's just as you say. Even though we're teaching others, all we do is memorize the words in the sutras and records and teach people what the old masters said. But, shameful though it is, we haven't actually realized enlightenment ourselves, so when we speak, our teaching is indeed like trying to scratch an itchy spot through your shoe—naturally, it's never satisfying. You understand us well,' they said, 'you can't be just an ordinary man!'

"So, without having managed to get anyone to confirm my experience for me, I returned home and went into retreat, shutting my door to the world. As I was observing the needs of the people then, considering the means to present my teaching and help to save them, I learned that [the Zen priest] Dōsha had come from China, having arrived at Nagasaki, where he was staying. On my teacher's instructions, I went to see Dōsha, and when I told him what I'd realized, he declared: 'You are a man who has transcended birth and death!' So, only at Dōsha's did I finally receive some small confirmation of my enlightenment. At that time, it was hard to find anyone who could testify with certainty to my experience, and I had quite a lot of trouble. That's why, thinking back now over what it was like for *me*, I come out like this every day to meet with all of you, ailing though I am. [47] If there's anyone here now who's experienced enlightenment—whoever he is—the only reason I've come out like this is so that I can be your witness. You people certainly are lucky! Since you have someone who can testify to your experience through and through, if there's anyone here who's been enlightened or who thinks he's understood this matter, step forward and let's hear from you. I'm ready to be your witness! However, if there's no one who's understood yet, listen to what I have to say, and realize conclusively. . . .

"Now, about what it means to realize conclusively that

what is unborn and marvelously illuminating is truly the Buddha Mind: Suppose ten million people got together and unanimously declared that a crow was a heron. A crow is black, without having to be dyed that way, just as a heron is white[48]—that's something we always see for ourselves and know for a fact. So even if, not only ten million people, but everyone in the land were to get together and tell you a crow was a heron, you still wouldn't be fooled, but remain absolutely sure of yourself. That's what it means to have a conclusive realization. Conclusively realize that what is unborn is the Buddha Mind and that the Buddha Mind is truly unborn and marvelously illuminating, and everything will be perfectly managed with the Unborn, so that, *whatever* people try to tell you, you won't let yourself be fooled by them. You won't accept other people's delusions.

"At the time I was young and first began to teach this true teaching of the Unborn, no one was able to understand. When they heard me, people seemed to think I was some sort of heretic or Christian,[49] so they were frightened off, and no one would go near me. But in time they realized they were wrong and saw that what I was teaching was the true Dharma itself. Now, instead of my original situation where no one would even go near me, I'm swamped with people coming to see me, anxious to meet me and listen to my teaching, after me continually, so that they don't leave me in peace even a single day! Things come in their own due time.

"From time to time in the forty years I've been here,[50] I've taught others this true teaching of the Unborn, and as a result this area has produced lots of people who are superior to teachers of Buddhism. So, for you people too, let the reward for your trouble in coming here all this way now be that you'll return home having experienced complete realization of the Dharma, thoroughly and conclusively realizing the principle of the Unborn without switching it for thoughts."

Growing up deluded

" . . . What everyone has from his parents innately is the Buddha Mind alone. But since your parents themselves fail to realize this, you become deluded too, and then display this delusion in raising your *own* children. Even the nursemaids and baby-sitters lose their temper, so that the people involved in bringing up children display every sort of deluded behavior, including stupidity, selfish desire and the [anger of] fighting demons.[51] Growing up with deluded people surrounding them, children develop a first-rate set of bad habits, becoming quite proficient at being deluded themselves, and turning into unenlightened beings. Originally, when you're born, you're without delusion. But on account of the faults of the people who raise you, someone abiding in the Buddha Mind is turned into a first-rate unenlightened being. This is something I'm sure you all know from your own experience.

"Your parents didn't give you any delusions whatever when you were born, no bad habits, no selfish desires. But afterward, once you'd come into the world, you picked up all different sorts of delusions, which then developed into bad habits, so that you couldn't help becoming deluded. That which you *didn't* pick up from outside is the Unborn Buddha Mind, and here no delusions exist. Since the Buddha Mind is marvelously illuminating, you're able to learn things, even to the point of thoroughly learning all sorts of deluded behavior. [At the same time,] since it's marvelously illuminating, when you hear this, you'll resolve *not* to be deluded, and from today on cease creating delusion, abiding in the Unborn Buddha Mind as it is. Just as before you applied yourself skillfully to picking up delusions and made yourself deluded, now you'll use the same skill to listen to this and *stop* being deluded—that's what a splendid thing the Buddha Mind is. Listen and you'll realize the preciousness of Buddha Mind. Then, since there's nothing that can take the place of this precious Buddha Mind, even if you *want* to be deluded, you won't be *able* to be anymore!

"It's because you don't realize the preciousness of Buddha Mind that you indulge in self-centeredness, creating delusions that do you harm. Yet those delusions are so precious to you that all of you actually *want* to become deluded, even at the risk of your own life! Foolish, isn't it? Unable to withstand the base impulses produced by your selfish desires, you become deluded. With all delusions it's the same.

"Everyone insists that the way he likes to behave is his innate character, so he can't do anything about it. He'll never tell you how, actually, he indulges in self-centeredness because of his selfish desires, holding on to those kinds of behavior he likes; instead, he tries to sound clever and talk about how it's all innate! To falsely accuse your own parents of something you never got from them is terribly unfilial. Is there anyone who's born a drunkard, a gambler or a thief—who's born with *any* sort of vice? No one's born that way. Once you pick up a taste for liquor, it promptly develops into a drinking habit, and then, because of selfish desire, you find yourself unable to stop, without realizing you've become deluded. It's only foolishness, so you've no cause to claim it's innate and pass off the blame on your parents!

"When you hear this, I want you all from today on to abide in the Unborn Buddha Mind just as it is—the Unborn Buddha Mind you have from your parents innately. Then, you won't create delusions about anything, and, since no delusions will remain, you'll be living buddhas from today forever after. Nothing could be more direct! You've all got to realize this conclusively."

Thirty days in the Unborn

"Everyone, do exactly as I'm telling you, and, following my instructions, start by trying to abide in the Unborn for thirty days. Learn to abide in the Unborn for thirty days, and from there on, even if you don't want to—whether you like it or not—you'll just naturally *have* to abide in the Unborn. You'll be a success at abiding in the Unborn! Since that which is unborn is the Buddha Mind, you'll be functioning with the Buddha Mind at all times. That way you'll be living buddhas here today, won't you? So listen to my teaching just as if today you were all born anew and starting afresh. When you've got some fixed notion, you won't take in what you hear. Listen as if you were newly born right now and it will be like hearing my teaching for the first time. If you don't have any fixed notion in your mind, at a single word you'll instantly understand and attain complete realization of the Dharma."

*   *   *

Ask me and I'll tell you

One day, the Master said: "I simply come out here like this each day to meet with you all; I haven't anything particular in mind I want to tell you. So if you've got anything to ask—whatever it is—everyone step right up and ask! Ask me and I'll tell you, no matter what it is. I've got nothing special in mind I want to say."

*   *   *

"The Kappa"

" . . . When I was young, there was a notorious thief in these parts called 'the Kappa,'[52] a fellow on the order of Kumasaka Chōhan,[53] who would boldly rob people on the highway, seizing their money. He had remarkable genius as a thief: when he caught sight of someone coming from across the way, he could tell exactly how much money he had on him and was never off by even a hair—that's what a formidable fellow he was. However, one day he got himself nabbed and served a long term in the prison at Osaka. The years passed, and then, because he was such an expert as a thief, he found himself at an advantage and was spared execution to become an informer for the police.[54] Later, he was excused from being an informer as well and became a free man. Afterward, he learned to carve Buddhist images, becoming a maker of Buddhist statues and settling in Osaka, an expert now at carving buddhas. Completely reversing his former wicked state of mind, he devoted himself to salvation, and ended his days absorbed in chanting the *nembutsu*.

"So, even such a notorious brigand as 'the Kappa,' once he'd reformed, ended his days in religious devotion. Where can you find anyone who steals because his karma is deep or his sins heavy? Stealing *is* the karma, stealing *is* the sin! If it weren't for stealing, that sin and karma couldn't exist. Whether you steal or whether you don't depends on the present state of your own mind, not on your past karma. And what I'm telling you now doesn't go only for stealing. Generally speaking, all delusions are just the same as stealing. Whether you're going to be deluded or you're not going to, all depends on the present state of your own mind. When you're deluded, you're an unenlightened being; when you're not deluded, you're a buddha. There's no special shortcut to being a buddha beyond this. Isn't it so? Everyone, realize this conclusively!"

*　　*　　*

Don't beat sleeping monks

On the opening day of *rōhatsu*,[55] the Master addressed the assembly: "In my place, our normal everyday life is meditation; so it's not like everywhere else where they announce: 'From today on, meditation!' and everyone specially hurls himself into frantic practice."

The Master then went on to say: "Once, while I was in Dōsha's assembly,[56] a monk was sleeping seated in meditation. Another monk there suddenly struck him, but I scolded him for doing this.

" 'Why should you hit someone who's pleasantly sleeping?' I said. 'When that monk is sleeping, do you think he's a different person!'

"I'm not encouraging people to sleep, but to hit them because they do is terribly wrong. Here in *my* place now, I don't allow that sort of thing. While I'm not encouraging people to sleep, I don't hit them or scold them for doing so. I don't scold or praise sleeping, and I don't scold or praise *not* sleeping. Whether people happen to be asleep or awake, just let them be as they are. When they're asleep, they're sleeping in the Buddha Mind they were awake in; when they're awake, they're awake in the Buddha Mind they were sleeping in. When people are asleep, they're sleeping in the Buddha Mind; when they're awake, they're awake in the Buddha Mind. They're *always* abiding in the Buddha Mind, and there's not a moment when they're ever abiding in anything else. So it's mistaken to think that when a person is asleep he turns into something different. If you believe that people abide in the Buddha Mind only when they're awake and that when they're asleep they turn into something different, that's not the ultimate truth, but an endless transformation.

"You're all exerting yourselves trying to realize buddha-hood, so if someone is sleeping, it's wrong to beat him or scold him. What you all have from your parents innately is the Unborn Buddha Mind alone and nothing else, so instead of trying to realize buddhahood, always abide in that Unborn Buddha Mind. Then, when you're asleep, you're sleeping in the Buddha Mind, and when you're awake, you're awake in the Buddha Mind; you're always a living buddha, and there's no time when you don't *remain* a buddha. Since you're a buddha all the time, there's no other special buddhahood for you to realize. Rather than trying to *become* a buddha, nothing could be simpler than taking the shortcut of *remaining* a buddha!"

Mind reading

Someone asked: "Everybody says your Reverence has the power to read people's minds.[57] Is it true?"

The Master said: "In my school, we don't have such extraordinary things. And even if we did, since the Buddha Mind is unborn, we wouldn't use them. When I'm speaking to you, I deal with your own selves, so you imagine I've got the power to read people's minds. But I haven't any mind-reading powers. I'm just the same as all of you. When you abide in the Unborn, you're at the source of the supernatural powers of all the buddhas, and without even having to *seek* supernatural power, all things are perfectly managed and smoothly dealt with. In the true teaching of the Unborn, you can manage everything by dealing with your own self, without bringing in all sorts of extraneous matters."

Moving ahead/sliding back

A certain man asked: "I've practiced as hard as I can, trying to advance without slipping back. But no matter what I do, the tendency to backslide is strong, and there are times when I regress. However much I try to advance, I only fall back again. How can I keep from regressing?"

The Master said: "Abide in the Unborn Buddha Mind! When you do, you won't need to bother about advancing or regressing. In fact, when you abide in the Unborn, trying to advance is to instantly regress from the place of the Unborn. The man of the Unborn has nothing to do with advancing or regressing, but always transcends them both."

Old wastepaper

A certain monk said: "For a long time now I've been working on the koan 'Hyakujō and the Wild Fox,'[58] but in spite of all my efforts, I still haven't solved it. I suspect this is simply because my practice isn't pure. I beg your Reverence to instruct me."

The Master said: "Here in my place we don't engage in such studies of old wastepaper![59] Since you haven't yet realized that what is unborn and marvelously illuminating is the Buddha Mind, let me tell you, and then everything will be straightened out. So listen carefully to what I say."

The Master then presented his teaching of the Unborn, just as usual. The monk, having listened attentively, profoundly acknowledged it, and thereafter is said to have distinguished himself as an outstanding figure.

Then, a monk who was [seated] nearby asked: "In that case, are the koans of the old masters useless and unnecessary?"

The Master said: "The responses of the old masters were only to shut off questions from individual students by confronting them immediately, face to face;[60] they have no particular usefulness [in themselves]. There's no way for me to say whether they're necessary or superfluous, helpful or useless.[61] When people just abide in the Unborn Buddha Mind, that's all there is to it, and there's no longer any way they can be sidetracked. So abide in the Unborn! In your case, you've been so carried away in sidetracking yourself, it's made you deluded. So give it up, and since that which is unborn and marvelously illuminating is the Buddha Mind and nothing else, abide in the Unborn Buddha Mind!"

* * *

Self-centeredness

One day, the Master addressed the assembly: "All delusions, without exception, are created as a result of self-centeredness. When you're free from self-centeredness, delusions won't be produced. For example, suppose your neighbors are having a quarrel: if you're not personally involved, you just hear what's going on and don't get angry. Not only do you not get angry, but you can plainly tell the rights and wrongs of the case—it's clear to you as you listen who's right and who's wrong. But let it be something that concerns you personally, and you find yourself getting involved with what the other party [says or does], attaching to it and obscuring the marvelously illuminating [function of the Buddha Mind]. Before, you could clearly tell wrong from right; but now, led by self-centeredness, you insist that your own idea of what's right is right, whether it is or not. Becoming angry, you thoughtlessly switch your Buddha Mind for a fighting demon, and everyone takes to arguing bitterly with each other.

"Because the Buddha Mind is marvelously illuminating, the traces of everything you've done are [spontaneously] reflected. It's when you *attach* to these reflected traces that you produce delusion. Thoughts don't actually exist in the place where the traces are reflected, and then arise. We retain the things we saw and heard in the past, and when these come up, they appear as traces and are reflected. Originally, thoughts have no real substance. So if they're reflected, just let them be reflected; if they arise, just let them arise; if they stop, just let them stop. As long as you're not *attaching* to these reflected traces, delusions won't be produced. So long as you're not attaching to them, you won't be deluded, and then, no matter how many traces are reflected, it will be just as if they weren't reflected at all. Even if a hundred, or a *thousand* thoughts spring up, it will be just the same as if they never arose. It won't be any problem for you—no thoughts to 'clear away,' no thoughts to 'cut off.' So understand this well!"

Bankei's Kannon

The principal object of worship at the Ryōmonji was a Kannon made by the Master.[62] Knowing this, when the Master was delivering a sermon, a monk from Ōshū[63] stood leaning against a pillar and asked:

"Is that image an old buddha or a new buddha?"

The Master replied: "How does it look to you?"

The monk said: "It looks to me like a new buddha."

The Master said: "If it looks to you like a new buddha, then it's a new buddha, and that's that; so what's the problem? Because you haven't understood that what is unborn is the Buddha Mind, you come and ask this sort of useless thing, thinking that's Zen. Rather than ask this kind of worthless stuff and disturb everyone, just keep quiet, take a seat, and listen carefully to what I'm saying."

Getting sidetracked

A layman from Izumo[64] presented himself for private instruction[65] with the Master and asked: "When one is enlightened like your Reverence, do the Three Worlds [of the past, present and future] really appear as if they were glimpsed in the palm of the hand?"

The Master said: "What you asked me just now was whether, when one is enlightened like myself, the Three Worlds appear as if glimpsed in the palm of the hand; is that correct?"

The layman said: "It is."

The Master said: "Is that question something you've been thinking over, or is it something that suddenly occurred to you just now to ask?"

The layman said: "Well, I didn't really form this question on the spur of the moment, but as I've been mulling it over and just happened to think of it now, I asked you about it."

The Master told him: "In that case, you needn't bother asking about *my* affairs. Your wanting to see the Three Worlds can wait. First, thoroughly examine your own self—what's really essential right here and now. Until you've examined your own self, however much I tell you about how things look [to *me*], you won't be recognizing it, seeing it or settling it for yourself, so you won't be convinced. And even if you did believe it, you still wouldn't be *proving* my words. Since you won't have seen the Three Worlds for yourself, it won't be of any use to you. When you thoroughly examine your own self, you'll know *for yourself* both the visible and invisible. There won't be any need for me to tell you, or for you to ask me. Without first of all thoroughly examining your own self—what's really essential right here and now—you come asking me extraneous questions about whether or not the Three Worlds can be seen, all of which can easily wait. It's just getting sidetracked, going off on a tangent; it's all irrelevant to you, like counting up my money for me without having even half a cent of your own. First off, listen closely to what I'm saying, and when you've really acknowledged it, today everything will be settled for you once and for all! So pay close attention and do just as I tell you, following my instructions. When you've acknowledged what I say and realized it conclusively, you'll be an instant living buddha here today. As for your question about whether one can see the Three Worlds or not, you won't have to carry it around to distant places, chasing about all over and asking others. Simply realize your mistake, and you'll stop side-tracking yourself, so listen closely to what I say."

The Master then presented his teaching of the Unborn, just as usual.

The layman, having heard it through, readily acknowledged it, and declaring, "How grateful I am!" withdrew.

*   *   *

Self-power/other-power

"My teaching isn't concerned with either self-power or other-power:[66] that which transcends both self-power and other-power, that's what my teaching is about. Let me prove this to you: While everyone is turned this way to hear me saying this, out back there may be sparrows chirping, crows cawing, the voices of men or women, or the sighing of the wind. But, without your deliberately trying to hear every one of those sounds, each of them comes to you clearly recognized and distinguished. It's not *you* doing the hearing, so it's not a matter of self-power. On the other hand, since you can't very well have someone else do your hearing for you, you couldn't call it other-power! So, that which isn't concerned with self-power *or* other-power but transcends them both is what my teaching is about. Isn't that right? When you listen this way with the Unborn, you transcend whatever there is. And all the rest of your activities are perfectly managed like this with the Unborn too. For the man who functions with the Unborn, whoever he may be, all things are perfectly managed. So, whoever he is, the man of the Unborn isn't concerned with either self-power or other-power, but transcends them both."

Dreams

A monk asked: "When I'm sleeping soundly, I have dreams. How is it that we have dreams? I'd like your opinion on this."

The Master said: "When a person is sound asleep he doesn't have dreams. When you have dreams, you're not sleeping soundly."

The monk was speechless.

Everybody has the Buddha Mind

The Master addressed the assembly:[67] "What I tell everyone is nothing but the fact that the Unborn Buddha Mind is marvelously illuminating. You're all endowed with the Buddha Mind, but since you don't know it, I'm telling you and trying to make you understand.

"Well, then, just what does it mean that everybody has the Buddha Mind? All of you came from home with the express intention of hearing what I've got to say, so you're supposed to be listening to the sermon. But, in the course of listening to my talk, if a dog barks outside the temple, you recognize it as the voice of a dog; if a crow caws, you know it's a crow; if you hear the voice of an adult, you know it's an adult; if you hear the voice of a child, you know it's a child. What I mean is that when you all left your homes to come here to the temple, you did so precisely in order to hear me speak this way; you didn't come with any preconceived idea that if, while I was talking, there were sounds of dogs and birds, children or grown-ups somewhere outside, you were deliberately going to try to hear them. Yet here in the meeting you recognize the noises of dogs and crows outside and the sounds of people talking; your eyes can distinguish red from white, and your nose tell good smells from bad. From the start, you had no deliberate intention of doing this, so you had no way to know which sounds, colors or smells you would encounter. But the fact that you recognize these things you didn't *expect* to see or hear shows you're seeing and hearing with the Unborn Buddha Mind. If outside the temple a dog barks, you know it's a dog; if a crow caws, you know it's a crow. Even though you're not deliberately trying to hear or not to hear these different sounds, you recognize each one the moment it appears, and this is proof of the Buddha Mind, unborn and marvelously illuminating. This not deliberately *trying* to see or hear is the Unborn. . . .

"I tell everyone how they're endowed with the Buddha Mind like this. From the time I was young, I devoted myself to realizing the Buddha Mind, going about everywhere engaging in religious practice, seeking out accomplished teachers and interviewing them, questioning them this way and that about my problem, but there wasn't one who could tell me what I had to know. The result was that I failed to get a clear understanding and struggled in all kinds of ways, doing zazen, living off in the mountains, punishing my body, but I was still in the dark about the matter of the Buddha Mind. Then, at last, when I was twenty-six, suddenly I hit on it, and ever since, I've been telling everyone how the Unborn Buddha Mind is marvelously illuminating, so that they can also understand. I doubt there are many people around who can give you this kind of detail!

"As I've told you, I finally realized this Buddha Mind after long years of religious practice. But the fact that all of you can easily come to know the Buddha Mind right at this meeting, in perfect comfort, without engaging in religious practice or punishing your bodies, means that your affinity with buddhahood is far deeper than mine was, and makes you lucky people indeed, each and every one! Having discovered that the Unborn Buddha Mind is marvelously illuminating, I've taught this everywhere, and many have understood. Of course, this Unborn Buddha Mind isn't anything I learned from my teacher—this Unborn is something I discovered for myself, and at every one of these meetings I teach according to my own realization. Since if I told it to you only once or twice you probably wouldn't understand, I tell it to you again and again. So if you've got any question about anything, just ask me, and I'll speak to you some more. . . .

"What is it I tell everyone? I only talk about the Unborn Buddha Mind you all intrinsically possess. The main thing is to realize this Buddha Mind. Originally, there isn't anything evil in you; but from just one little slip, you switch the Buddha Mind for thoughts. Take a thief, for example: At first, he pinches a few trifles, and then thinks: 'I got hold of these things without even having to put up any cash; I'm sure there's no handier way [to make a living]!' After that, he becomes a confirmed and reckless thief, is inevitably found out, collared, bound, jailed and [led off to be] crucified. But then, confronted with the punishment for his crimes, he forgets all about the evils he committed and rails against the innocent officials who must carry out his execution, protesting that what he's done doesn't deserve such harsh treatment and that it's heartlessly cruel besides! Terribly mistaken, isn't it? This is how people switch their precious Buddha Mind for the realms of hungry ghosts and fighting demons—it all begins from one little slip.

"I also have a temple in Kyoto, at Yamashina,[68] and when I'm staying there I go into the city every day. Awadaguchi[69] lies along my way, and at Awadaguchi is a place where criminals are crucified and their heads gibbeted before the prison gates. Having to pass by there frequently, I'd see this sort of thing from time to time.

"In Edo, the Criminal Magistrate is a man named Lord Kōide Ōzumi.[70] I'm on friendly terms with him, and whenever I'd visit at his mansion, I'd see various criminals led out, confronted by the officers, bound and tied and put to the torture, suffering the most terrible agony. At that moment, these criminals quite forgot their own mischief was to blame and berated the officers, who were in no way at fault, as if it were all *their* doing. I often witnessed this. Afterwards, seeing how things were, I'd make sure I visited only on Official Days of Abstinence,[71] as on these days such criminals weren't brought to the mansion. This is an example of how, from one little slip, people thoughtlessly change the Buddha Mind for a hell-dweller. Everyone, grasp this clearly! When it comes to what you all have from your parents innately, there's not a single thing you've got except the Buddha Mind. So take great care not to create delusions and bad habits, which result from self-centeredness and selfish desires that you do *not* have innately. It's to illustrate this that I've told you about the criminals. . . .

"When your parents gave you life, there wasn't a trace of selfish desire, bad habits or self-centeredness. But from the age of four or five you picked up the mean things you saw other people do and the bad things you heard them say, so that gradually as you matured, growing up badly, you developed selfish desire, which in turn produced self-centeredness. Deluded by this self-centeredness, you then proceeded to create every sort of evil. If it weren't for being centered on yourself, delusions wouldn't arise. When they don't arise, that's none other than abiding in the Unborn Buddha Mind. Apart from this, there's no buddha, so if there's anything you people don't understand, come along and ask me, no matter what it is. There's no need to feel any hesitation in asking about this. This is different from asking about worldly concerns of the moment—it's a matter of eternity! So if you've got any doubts, better come ask me right now. I can't be sure of meeting you all again, so take this opportunity to ask me about whatever puzzles you, and when you've thoroughly grasped how the Buddha Mind is unborn and marvelously illuminating, each of you will have his reward."

Having thus instructed the assembly, the Master mounted the altar platform[72] to perform the closing ceremonies, and when he had finished, he said: "I'm going back inside now. Today's crowd was quite a big one, so, to avoid a rush, everyone please leave in an orderly fashion, and, above all, take your time going so there won't be any mishaps."

Being living buddhas

"What has brought this vast throng here like this since daybreak, hoping to hear what I've got to say, is none other than the Unborn Buddha Mind. The way you've all gathered here since early this morning, unless you'd felt the sermon was something really unusual, you'd never have shown this sort of resolve. Well, then, among those of you who've come to this meeting, all those who've reached the age of fifty have lived for fifty years without realizing you had the Buddha Mind right within yourself, while those who are thirty have failed to realize this truth for thirty years up till today—you've all been passing the months and years in a daze. But at our meeting today when you thoroughly grasp that each of you has the Unborn Buddha Mind right within himself, from today on you'll live in the Buddha Mind and be living buddhas forever after. What I'm telling you all is simply to make you realize that the Unborn Buddha Mind is marvelously illuminating. When you've thoroughly realized this, from then on forever after you'll possess a buddha's body no different from Shaka's[73] and never again fall into the Three Evil Realms. However, even if you grasp the Unborn Buddha Mind when I explain it to you here like this, once you go back home, things you see and hear may start up your angry mind again. And then, even if it's only a tiny bit of anger, your sin will be a million times worse than it was *before* you'd heard me tell you about the Unborn Buddha Mind! You'll switch the Unborn Buddha Mind you learned about now for hell-dwellers, beasts and hungry ghosts, transmigrating forever.

"I'm sure there's not a person present who objects to becoming a buddha. That's why I'm here preaching to you all. Grasp things clearly, and from today on you're living buddhas. Even if I were to urge you all, 'Forget about becoming buddhas—just fall into hell!' I doubt there would be a single one of you who'd actually volunteer to go! The proof of this is that, in order to come to this meeting and hear my sermon, you roused yourselves in the dark of night, traveling here and jostling for space in this huge crowd, accepting all the hardships to listen to my talk. Isn't it because you all wanted to become buddhas? Since you have this sort of resolve, from here on you should take great care in everything you do. . . .

" 'Just what sort of thing *is* this Unborn Buddha Mind?' you're probably wondering. While all of you here are turned this way intent on hearing what I'm saying, if outside the temple there's the barking of a dog or the cry of some tradesman peddling his wares, even though you're not trying to hear these things in the course of the sermon, each of

the different sounds is heard—the dog's bark, the tradesman's cry; that's hearing with the Unborn, the dynamic
function of the Buddha Mind. Let me give you an example. The Buddha Mind, unborn and marvelously illuminating, is like a bright mirror. A mirror reflects whatever
is in front of it. It's not deliberately *trying* to reflect things,
but whatever comes before the mirror, its color and form
are sure to appear. Likewise, when the object being reflected is removed, the mirror isn't deliberately trying *not*
to reflect it, but when it's taken away it doesn't appear in
the mirror. The Unborn Buddha Mind is just like this. It's
natural that you see and hear things, whatever they are,
when you deliberately *try* to see and hear them; but when
you see and hear things that you hadn't originally *anticipated* seeing or hearing, it's through the dynamic function
of the Buddha Mind that every one of you has. That's
what's meant by the Unborn Buddha Mind. Now that I've
given you my instruction on the Unborn in such a way
that all of you can understand, if after this you still don't
grasp it, then whether you've listened to one thousand
sermons or ten thousand, it won't make any difference.
Even if it's only *one* sermon, the person who realizes this
Buddha Mind that everyone intrinsically possesses is a living tathagata from that moment on!

"To give you another example, suppose there's someone traveling here to Marugame from Takamatsu,[74] and
he doesn't know the way. There's another person who does
know it, and when the traveler asks him, he explains precisely what route to follow and, memorizing this thoroughly, the traveler goes just as he'd been told and arrives
here without any problem. The same way, when you all
grasp exactly what I'm saying now, from that moment on
you'll abide in the Buddha Mind just as it is. On the other
hand, if you fail to do so, it's just as if you were able to
learn the road to Marugame, but didn't go as you'd been
told and headed for some place else. That's why you'd

better listen closely to what I say. I can't be sure I'll be back here again to talk to you; and even if you hear sermons somewhere else, I doubt there's anyone who's going to make a special point of explaining to you how this Buddha Mind is unborn and marvelously illuminating. So if you think the sermon I'm giving makes sense, be on your guard to stop stirring up all kinds of thoughts, and put an end to your transmigrating. If you fail to realize buddhahood now, you'll never again be born into this human world, not even in ten thousand kalpas,[75] so do your utmost to conclusively realize the Unborn Buddha Mind, and don't be deluded. Then, from today you men will be men abiding in the Buddha Mind, and you women will be women abiding in the Buddha Mind, all without being deluded. That's none other than buddhahood, none other than enlightenment.

"I can tell you something about this matter of women's Buddha Mind. I understand that women feel very distressed hearing it said that they can't become buddhas. But it simply isn't so! How is there any difference between men and women? Men are the Buddha Body,[76] and women are the Buddha Body too. You shouldn't entertain any doubts of this sort. When you thoroughly grasp the Unborn, then, in the Unborn, there's no difference whether you're a man or a woman. Everyone is the Buddha Body.

"You women, listen closely now. While, in terms of physical form, men and women are obviously different, in terms of the Buddha Mind there's no difference at all. Don't be misled by appearances! The Buddha Mind is identical; it makes no distinction between men and women.

"Let me prove this to you. There's quite a crowd of people here at this meeting, but when they hear the sound of a drum or a gong outside the temple, do you suppose the women mistake the sound of the gong for that of the drum, the sound of the drum for that of the gong? Do you really think there's any difference between the way the men are hearing these things and the way the women hear them? There's absolutely no difference at all. Now, every-one, is this true only for 'men and women'? In this hall we have young people and old, monks and householders, men and women, all here mingled together; but when it comes to hearing the sound of the gong or the drum, can you say the old people hear it this way, the young ones hear it that way? Can you tell the difference in the way the monks hear it, the way the lay people hear it, the way the men hear it, the way the women hear it? The fact that there's no differ-ence at all [proves that what's involved] is none other than the One Identical Buddha Mind that everyone intrinsically possesses. So this talk about 'men's and women's' is noth-ing but names of traces produced by your thoughts. Before these traces get produced, in the realm of the Unborn, there's nothing about 'men' or 'women.' And since that's how it is, as there's no difference between men's Buddha Mind and women's Buddha Mind, you shouldn't harbor any such doubts.

"Suppose you are staying continually in the Unborn, abiding in the Buddha Mind just as it is and forgetting any distinctions between men and women, when suddenly you see or hear something [disturbing], someone says nasty things about you, or thoughts of clinging and craving arise and you attach to them: you'll carelessly switch the Buddha Mind for thoughts, and then claim it's because you're only a wretched woman, or some such thing. Without being deluded by your physical form, thoroughly grasp this One Way of the Unborn, and [you'll see that] not only men and women, but the buddhas of the past and those of the future are all the identical One Buddha Mind. There's no reason that women should be a special case and not be able to realize buddhahood too.

"If there really *were* some reason that women couldn't become buddhas, just what do you think I would have to gain by deceiving you all, lying to you and insisting they *can*, misleading everyone in this big crowd? If it were a

fact that women couldn't realize buddhahood, and I told
you that they really *could*, deceiving every person here, I'd
be sure to land in hell well before all of you! Just because
I longed to realize buddhahood, from the time I was young
I engaged in hard and painful practice; so now do you
suppose I'd want to get punished for lying to you all and
land up in hell? What I'm telling you is no lie. I want you
ladies to grasp it clearly and, from here on, feeling fully
assured, pass your days in the Unborn Buddha Mind. . . .

"Even in *evil* people, the Unborn Mind isn't missing.
When you reverse their evil mind, it's none other than
Buddha Mind. Let me tell you how even an evil person
has the Buddha Mind: Suppose two men are traveling
together from here to Takamatsu. One of them is evil and
the other is good, but both of them, without thinking of
good or evil, just walk along, chatting with one another
about this or that as they go. If there's something along the
road, without either of them deliberately trying to see it,
whatever there is on either side appears to both the eyes of
the good man and to those of the bad. Suppose some
horses or cows should come toward them: both the good
man and the bad would move aside and make their way
around. Even though they hadn't anticipated doing so, as
they go along chatting together, both of them simply move
aside to get through. If there's some spot they have to leap
across, both of them will take a leap; if there's a river,
they'll both ford it. Even though he hadn't planned to do
so, the good man, as you'd expect, moves aside and makes
his way past whatever obstacles he encounters. But while
you might expect that the evil man *wouldn't* do exactly the
same as the good one—ducking out of the way of things,
leaping ditches and fording streams without any anticipa-
tion—what he does is, in fact, no different from what the
good man does.

"I've told you this as an example of how even an evil
person is endowed with the Unborn Buddha Mind. Each

of you too, up till now, has been an evil person, consumed by every sort of clinging and craving, preoccupied with anger and rage, transmigrating and switching your Buddha Mind for fighting demons and hungry ghosts. But now that I've explained this Unborn Buddha Mind to you to-day, if you grasp it clearly, your own mind of clinging and craving, anger and rage will instantly become the Unborn Buddha Mind, and you'll never lose this Buddha Mind, not in ten thousand kalpas. Since you'll be abiding in this Buddha Mind, from today on you yourselves will be living tathagatas. But make no mistake; if you lose out on the Buddha Mind now, you won't attain buddhahood in ten thousand or even one *hundred* thousand kalpas, so you'd better grasp things clearly!

"Even if your previously ingrained bad habits should lead you to attach to things that come your way, so that thoughts temporarily arise, the man who is secure in his faith will neither attach to nor reject these thoughts—in the twinkling of an eye he'll easily go right back to the buddhahood of the Unborn! Even with the buddhas and patriarchs, it wasn't that they were completely without thoughts from the start. But since they didn't get involved with them and, just like little children, didn't continue them any further, it was the same as if the thoughts didn't arise. That's why they remained free from thoughts.

"Now, when thoughts don't arise, the marvelously il-luminating dynamic function of the Buddha Mind won't manifest itself, so the arising of thoughts is, in fact, the dynamic function of the marvelously illuminating Buddha Mind. Both my explaining these things to you and your taking them in, too, are all due to everyone's having that which is marvelously illuminating within the Buddha Mind. Isn't this a direct and precious thing? To take something so precious, arouse all kinds of thoughts and with them create the Three Evil Realms of hell-dwellers, beasts and hungry ghosts, so that even right in this life you're pulled along by that [evil] karma—it's really pitiful to think how people suffer like this, morning to night. So grasp this clearly, realize once and for all that dealing with everything by stirring up thoughts only makes you suffer; and, without switching your One Buddha Mind for thoughts that are *not* innately yours, pass your days always in the Unborn Buddha Mind.

"I'll be going back inside now. Everyone please take your time leaving."

Servants, samurai, husbands and wives

" . . . When you observe the world at large, if there's someone with a certain skill in which he excels, no matter what it is, everyone will praise him: 'He's really talented!' they'll declare. But the bigoted person, on hearing this, will say: 'Well, he may be good at this particular thing, but he's also got such-and-such *bad* points . . .' thus managing to denigrate even his abilities. There's no two ways about it: that's the bigotry of the arrogant evildoer, isn't it? With people like this, if someone they're partial to has a little talent, even if it's talent no one else has ever heard of, they'll stand up alone and praise him to the skies. 'Bravo!' they exclaim, 'Well done! A real virtuoso!' You find lots of people like this. Isn't that sort of thing terribly wrong? We should join gladly in praising those whom others praise, and, hearing of another's happiness, we should rejoice just as if the happiness were our own. This is the way things ought to be. Such a person is an illumined man who doesn't obscure the Buddha Mind. But if, in response to what you see and hear, there's any arrogance or bigotry, you change the Buddha Mind with which you're endowed for a hell-dweller. . . .

"When you leave behind your anger, clinging, craving and self-centeredness, even when it comes to your servants, you won't treat them harshly but will show them kindness. Just because you hire someone and pay him a salary is no reason to beat him or make him do unreasonable things! Even with your servants, you shouldn't think of them as separate or unrelated to you. Suppose right now your own son were being disobedient. If instead of your son disobeying you it had been an outsider, how incensed you'd be! But since you realize it's your own son, you manage to put up with it, right? What's more, whatever sort of nasty thing you'd tell your own son to do, since it's in the family he probably wouldn't resent it too much; but with a servant, who is unrelated to you, his resentment is bound to be different from your son's. Scolding people heedlessly, flying into a rage—till now it's all been a great mistake. Till now, you didn't understand the principle behind this, so you just went along thoughtlessly, believing that anger and rage were the natural way of things in the human world. But now that you've heard about the Unborn Buddha Mind each of you has innately, from here on you'd better keep from doing it any harm.

"It may seem to you somehow that I'm speaking like this at the request of the servants—but it really isn't so! Even when it comes to a rude servant, no matter how bad he is, what I'm telling you all is not to lose your temper senselessly and harm the Buddha Mind. . . .

"In the world, one finds certain kinds of men who do things halfheartedly. Unlike men, however, women are sincere. It's true they're also more foolish than men in some ways. But when you tell them that by doing evil you fall into hell, they don't doubt it in the slightest; and when you teach them that, while doing evil will land you in hell, doing good will make you a buddha, they wholeheartedly resolve to become buddhas, and their faith deepens all the more. When they hear what I'm teaching about the Unborn, their faith is roused, and that's why women, being sincere, will realize buddhahood more readily than

men with their phony cleverness. So make up your minds
that you're going to become buddhas now!

"Everyone is probably thinking: 'Here he is just telling
us, "Watch out all the time—don't lose your temper! don't
be greedy!" But if we were doing this and someone came
along and remarked, "Why, what big fools these people
are!" we surely couldn't bring ourselves to tell him, "Certainly, we *are* fools!" '

"Of course, such things do happen; but a person who
calls another a fool, even when he's not, is a fool himself.
So with people like this, just let it go and don't bother
about it any further.

"However, if a samurai were being addressed with such
disrespectful talk, there'd be no question of his tolerating
it. Let me give you an example. Nowadays there are lots
of people who own high-priced ceramics—flower vases
and Korean teabowls.[77] I don't own anything of this sort
myself, but when I see the people who do, they take the
ceramics and wrap them round and round with soft cotton
and crepe and stick them in a box, which makes good
sense. If a costly ceramic strikes against something hard,
it's sure to break, so to keep these ceramics from breaking
by wrapping them in cotton and crepe is surely a judicious
measure. The samurai's mind is just like this. To begin
with, samurai always place honor above all else. If there's
even a single word of disagreement between them, they
can't let it pass without calling it to account—such is the
way of the samurai. Once a single word is challenged,
there's no going back. So a samurai always keeps the 'hard'
parts of his mind under wraps, swathed in cotton and
crepe, and from the start takes the greatest care to avoid
'striking against' abrasive people. Everyone would do well
always to be careful about this. Once anyone has challenged his words, the samurai is bound to kill him. You'd
better grasp this clearly.

"Then there's the sort of killing that occurs when a

samurai throws himself before his lord and cuts down an attacker. This serves to destroy evildoers and pacify the realm and constitutes the regular vocation of the samurai, so for a warrior this sort of thing is not considered to be murder. But to kill another simply scheming for your own personal ends, stirring up selfish desires as a result of self-centeredness—this is murder indeed. It shows disloyalty to your lord, unfiliality to your parents, and changes the Buddha Mind for a fighting demon. On the other hand, in circumstances when one must die for one's lord, to fail to die, to run away and behave like a coward, is switching the Buddha Mind for an animal. Birds and beasts don't have the sort of intelligence people do, so they can't understand the proper way to act; they don't know the meaning of honor and simply flee from place to place trying to stay alive. But when a samurai, similarly, fails to understand the meaning of honor and runs away, not even showing shame before his fellow warriors, that's just like being an animal.

"In Edo, I also have a temple,[78] located in Azabu on the edge of the city. There was once a servant who'd been with me for quite some time and had developed a certain religious feeling. I suppose that as he constantly watched the behavior of the monks, this sort of thing had naturally occurred. It happened that one day, toward dusk, this man was sent on an errand by some of my students. His route led through the outskirts of the city, past certain areas with homes and others that were totally uninhabited. In these desolate spots, swordsmen would often lie in wait to test their blades on unsuspecting travelers,[79] and with no one about after dark, it wasn't safe to be there. But when the others tried to stop him, pleading, 'It's dangerous, don't go!' he refused to listen, and went off, telling them, 'I'll be back.'

"On his way home, the sun had gone down, and one of these streetcorner assassins happened to be waiting in his usual spot. He pushed deliberately into the servant, drew the sword at his side and exclaimed: 'You touched me with your sleeve! I won't let you by!'

"The servant replied: 'My sleeve did not touch you.'

"And then, without even thinking, he prostrated himself three times. Whereupon, strange to tell, the samurai sheathed the sword that was already poised to kill, and said: 'Well, you're a peculiar fellow! I'll let you off. Go on!'

"Thus, he managed to escape disaster.

"Meanwhile, a merchant who just then chanced to be passing saw what was happening and ran for safety into an adjacent tea shop, taking furtive peaks at what was going on. As he waited there wondering, 'Is he killing him now? *Now* is he going to kill him?' the servant appeared before him.

" 'You really had a narrow escape!' said the merchant. 'How'd you ever happen to think of bowing like that?'

"The servant told him: 'I live in a temple, and the people there are always making three bows. Just now, I decided, "Well, if he's going to kill me, let him kill me!" And, without even thinking, I just automatically made the usual three bows. "You're a peculiar fellow," he said, "I'll let you off. Go on!" And I was able to continue on my way.'

"That's what the servant told me.

" 'Even this,' I said to him, 'even your escape from an inescapable predicament, when you come right down to it, was because you always kept your faith.' And having heard how the heart of even a brutal wayside assassin was moved, I'm sure there isn't anyone who can doubt the Buddhadharma.

"As I travel about everywhere, I come across all sorts of different things. I also have a temple at Ōzu in Iyo,[80] and I generally go there and spend some time each year. The Ōzu temple is nothing like this. It's a huge structure. When I'm there, throngs of visitors pack the temple, and there's

one hall reserved for women and another just for men. In
Ōzu, we have four ushers—two for the women and two
for the men—who give directions so there won't be any
unseemly scrambling, and everyone listens respectfully.
All the local country people come from two or three *ri*[81]
around.

"Once there was a fellow from Ōzu who gave his
daughter in marriage to a man whose home was in the
countryside some two *ri* away. His mother lived with them,
and a son was born, but the couple always got on badly
and never ceased quarreling. Eventually, they had a terrible row, and the wife walked out, handing their only
child to her husband and announcing that she was returning to her parents.

"But the husband, clutching the child in his arms,
declared: 'If you go back to your parents, I'll throw this
child in the river!'

"The woman said: 'Fine! He's your child, and now I'm
letting you *have* him, so go ahead and throw him in the
river, get rid of him if you want to—I don't care!'

"Then, the husband told her: 'You may be going home
to your parents, but you're not taking back so much as a
scrap of clothing or household belongings!'[82]

"She replied: 'Once I'm out of this house, I don't *care*
about that clothing and household stuff!' And so saying,
she left and set off for Ōzu.

"Just then, she happened to notice a group of people
on their way to hear my sermon, so instead of continuing
to her parents, she joined the crowd and came to my
temple. She listened carefully to what I said that day. Well,
when my talk was over, everyone dispersed, and on the
way home, this woman happened to meet a man who was
a neighbor of her parents.

"'What's brought you here?' he asked her.

"She told him: 'This morning my husband and I had a
fight. I'd come this far when I noticed a crowd on their

way to the temple. It looked as if there would be a sermon, and the happy thought came to me that this was a good opportunity and I ought to join them. So, instead of proceeding to my parents, I went along to the temple. Everything in the sermon today applied to me personally. I feel so terribly ashamed! My leaving my husband's house today was due to my own wrongmindedness. My husband didn't want me to go. He tried saying all kinds of things to me and, together with my mother-in-law, attempted to stop me, but I persisted in my senseless outrage and finally outraged my husband and mother-in-law as well. However, the sermon today made me see how wrong I was, so I won't be going back to my parents after all. From here, I'll return home to my husband and beg forgiveness for the wrong I've done, humble myself before them both and also tell them about this wonderful sermon; for unless I encourage them as well to take an interest in salvation, my having heard it won't be truly worthwhile.'

"The neighbor remarked: 'How can you go back home alone after fighting with your husband and coming all this way? First, go to your parents' place; then, I'll go back to your husband's with you and see that your return works out all right.'

" 'No, no,' the woman said, 'it doesn't matter how it's going to work out. Since, after all, it was I who behaved badly, it's up to me to make up to them both and see that everything comes right. Besides, if this wonderful sermon remained for my hearing alone, it wouldn't be worthwhile. When I've shared it with them both and encouraged them to take an interest in salvation, only then will my having heard it be truly meaningful.'

"As the two of them walked along speaking this way, they were overheard by the people around them coming from the temple.

" 'What a remarkable person this woman is!' they marveled. 'Today, after hearing a single sermon, she repents her errors. What extraordinary behavior for a mere woman! This other person certainly spoke ignorantly. To try to dissuade her from going back alone, and to have *him* straighten things out for her return—what sort of business would that be! Since he's from Ōzu, he must have heard that sermon over and over, but, still, what bad advice he hands out!'

"In this fashion, those who'd been able to hear what had happened rebuked the man, and told the woman who had announced that she was going home: 'Your attitude really is admirable! Hurry home right away!'

" 'Yes, I *will*!' she replied, and returned.

"That day, I'd been invited to visit an Ōzu clansman, and while I was there, a crowd of acquaintances came by.

" 'Your sermon today caused a miracle!' they told me, all of them at once blurting out this story.

"Afterwards, I learned what happened when the woman went back to her husband.

"Returning as she'd intended, she told them both:[83] 'Even though neither of you ordered me out, my own wrongheadedness made me go against your wishes and leave home. Yet, since my decision to return to my parents led me to Ōzu, my leaving home today must itself have been the result of some karmic affinity with Buddhism. On my way, I met a crowd of people traveling to the temple, and, joining them, I went along. When I listened to the sermon, there wasn't a thing that didn't apply to me personally. As I listened, I realized how wrong my own attitude had been, and instead of going on to my parents, I came straight home from the temple. It was my own wrongmindedness that made you both angry with me. From here on, I'll obey you in everything, so if you're angry with me now, go ahead and satisfy your anger—do anything to me you want! No matter how trying things may be for me, I won't bear you any resentment at all, so I hope you'll both forgive me.'

"Like the honest folk they were, when they heard this,

both husband and mother-in-law declared: 'It was you who got yourself upset over nothing and ran out on your own, even though no one had told you to go. Now that you've realized you were mistaken and come back, how could we hold it against you!'

"So they were happy to have her back again, and everything turned out for the best. Thereafter, the woman was scrupulously obedient to her husband, with whom she lived in perfect harmony, and was respectful toward her mother-in-law as well, looking after the meals and telling them from time to time about the marvelous sermon she'd heard. Finally, she prevailed upon them both, so that while I was staying [in the area], the three of them would often come together to hear me.

"For people who have an affinity like this with Buddhism to be freed of their quarrels and resentments by a single sermon—even if they're only ignorant folk without any sort of understanding—certainly shows a wonderful attitude, don't you agree? I've been telling you this with the idea that if all of you, too, hear these things, you're sure to form an instant affinity of your own. Because the Buddha Mind is unborn and marvelously illuminating, even a mere woman, without any sort of understanding, can find herself relying on the Buddha Mind. So all you people as well, from here on, should constantly summon up your faith in order to abide in the Unborn Buddha Mind!

"Today's talk was long, and you're probably all worn out, so let's stop here. Everyone take your time leaving, and please come again tomorrow."

"Buddha" Magoemon

" . . . Well, then, let me tell you something about the marvelous workings of the Buddha Mind. About thirty years ago there was a fellow who became a disciple of mine, [a merchant] who outdid everyone else in selling his goods, frequently turning a handsome profit, so that people all began to call him 'Thief Magoemon.'[84] Whenever he'd pass by, everyone would point to him and say: 'There's that Thief Magoemon!' Still, as he was clever at turning a profit, outdoing all the rest, later on things went well for him—he got himself a house, made money—and from that time on, he often came to my place. I told him: 'If people are calling you an outrageous thief, something must be wrong. Particularly when someone who's coming regularly to this temple gets called such bad names by everyone and has everybody talking about him, there's no two ways about it—it's his own fault!'

"When I'd taken him to task like this, Magoemon said to me: 'If I went to people's places and stole things, or cut my way into their storerooms, I'd certainly feel ashamed; but I'm not stealing like that. And I'm hardly the only one around who's making a profit in business. Besides, the people who are slandering me are mostly merchants themselves, but since they can't turn a profit like I do, unfortunately you end up hearing bad things about me. After all, the whole point of doing business is to make a profit. . . .' And going on in this vein, he remained unconcerned.

"Later on, I don't know what came over him, but he turned his affairs over to his nephew and even distributed all the money he'd accumulated among his family, coming to me and asking to receive the tonsure. I told him: 'If it were anyone else, there'd certainly be some question in my mind, but in your case, as someone who's always had a bad reputation, it shows a splendid resolve.' So saying, I made him a monk right away.

"From then on, he gradually deepened his faith and became a man of faith. And what does this show? That what's called the Buddha Mind possesses a marvelously illuminating dynamic function. Not thirty days after this fellow had become a monk, everyone had already taken to calling him '*Buddha* Magoemon!' That's how it goes, so I want you all to grasp this clearly. There's nothing in the world so precious as the Buddha Mind. Since you're all trying to realize the Unborn Buddha Mind, you can't get by without understanding this conclusively. I don't go telling you: 'It's no good unless you perform this practice!' 'Observe the precepts!' 'Read the sutras and records!' 'Do zazen!' Because the Buddha Mind is present in each one of you, there's no question of my *giving* you the Buddha Mind. Listening closely to this sermon, realize the Buddha Mind that each of you has right within himself, and from today on you're abiding in the Unborn Buddha Mind. Once you've affirmed the Buddha Mind that everyone has innately, you can all do just as you please: if you want to read the sutras, read the sutras; if you feel like doing zazen, do zazen; if you want to keep the precepts, take the precepts; even if it's chanting the *nembutsu* or the *daimoku*,[85] or simply performing your allotted tasks—whether as a samurai, a farmer, an artisan or a merchant[86]—*that* becomes your *samādhi*.[87] All I'm telling you is: 'Realize the Buddha Mind that each of you has from your parents innately!' What's essential is to realize the Buddha Mind each of you has, and simply abide in it with faith. . . ."

Like little children of three or four

The Master instructed the assembly: "As you've all been hearing me say, everyone has the innate Buddha Mind, so all you need to do is abide in the Unborn just as it is. However, [following] the ways of the world, you get into bad habits in life and switch the Buddha Mind for the wretched realm of hungry ghosts with its clinging and craving. Grasp this thoroughly and you'll always abide in the Unborn Buddha Mind. But if, wishing to realize the Unborn, you people try to *stop* your thoughts of anger and rage, clinging and craving from arising, then by stopping them you divide one mind into two. It's as if you were pursuing something that's running away. As long as you deliberately try to stop your rising thoughts, the thought of trying to stop them wars against the continually arising thoughts themselves, and there's never an end to it. To give you an example, it would be like washing away blood with blood. Of course, you might get out the original blood; but the blood after that would stick, and the red never go away. Similarly, the original angry thoughts that you were able to stop may have come to an end, but the subsequent thoughts concerned with your stopping them won't *ever* cease.

" 'Well,' you may wonder, 'then what *can* I do to stop them?' Even if suddenly, despite yourself and wholly unawares, rage or anger should appear, or thoughts of clinging and craving arise, just let them come—don't develop them any further, don't attach to them. Without concerning yourself about whether to stop your rising thoughts or not to stop them, just don't bother with them, and then there's nothing else they can do *but* stop. You can't have an argument with the fence if you're standing there all alone! When there's no one there to fight with, things can't help but simply come to an end of themselves.

"Even when all sorts of thoughts do crop up, it's only for the time being while they arise. So, just like little children of three or four who are busy at play, when you don't continue holding onto those thoughts and don't cling to any [particular] thoughts, whether they're happy or sad, not thinking about whether to stop or not to stop them— why, that's nothing else but abiding in the Unborn Buddha Mind. So keep the one mind *as* one mind. If you always have your mind like this, then, whether it's good things or bad, even though you're neither trying *not* to think them nor to stop them, they can't help but just stop of themselves. What you call anger and joy you produce entirely yourself due to the strength of your self-centeredness, the result of selfish desire. Transcend all thoughts of attachment and these thoughts can't help but perish. This 'perishing' is none other than the *Im*perishable. And that which is imperishable is the Unborn Buddha Mind.

"At any rate, the main thing is always to be mindful of the Unborn Buddha Mind and not go cooking up thoughts of this or that on the ground of the Unborn, attaching to things that come your way, changing the Buddha Mind for thoughts. As long as you don't waver in this, no thoughts will arise, whether good or bad, and so, of course, there won't be any need to try to stop them, either. Then, aren't you neither creating nor destroying? That's nothing but the Unborn and Imperishable Buddha Mind, so you'd better grasp this clearly!"

Getting angry

"Looking around me, I see that we have an even larger crowd than usual this morning, so probably a lot of you didn't hear the talk I just gave. All those who heard it should leave at this point and give their places to those who didn't."

When those present had changed places and seated themselves, a certain man brought forward a question he wished to ask the Master.

"In your sermons," he said, "you always state that, getting into bad habits in life, we switch the Buddha mind for evil thoughts. Hearing you, I realize that doing this is wrong. Still, I'm a townsman, my business is trade, and things people say make me angry or annoyed. Inside me, I don't harbor any evil thoughts of anger or annoyance, but other people often *get* me angry, whether it's my wife and children or my servants. After hearing your sermon, I realized doing this was wrong and tried to put an end to it. But if I stop those angry thoughts, they only come up again, and there's no end to them after all. What can I do, then, to stop them?"

The Master replied: "The fact is, you *want* to get angry, so you're *getting* yourself mad. If you hadn't the least bad thought to begin with, no matter how much others provoked you, you surely wouldn't get angry. But if, in you, feelings of anger and annoyance have already been formed, then, even though [the other people] don't set out deliberately to say things to make you mad, you get carried away by the force of your own self-centeredness, lose your temper and insist, 'I don't say anything that's untrue or improper!' Your thoughts create the karma of the Three Evil Realms, while your demonic mind torments you. This is the fiery cart[88] of self and self-created karma.

"Outside, hell, hungry ghosts, karma, demons and fiery carts simply don't exist. What's more, to try to stop your rising thoughts, holding them back and suppressing them, is a bad idea. The original, innate Buddha Mind is one alone—it's never two. But when you try to stop your rising anger, [your mind] is split between your angry thoughts and your thoughts of stopping them. It's as if you're chasing after someone who is running away, except that you're both the runner and the one pursuing him as well! Let me give you an example of what I mean: You can busy yourself sweeping under a tree with thick [autumn] foliage; but since the tree's leaves will keep scattering down from above, even if, for the moment, you manage to get things neatly swept away, more leaves will only come falling later on, won't they? In the same way, even if you stop your original thoughts of anger, the subsequent thoughts involved with the stopping of them will never come to an end. So the idea of trying to stop [your thoughts] is wrong. Since that's how it is, when you no longer bother about those rising thoughts, not trying either to stop them or not to stop

them, why, that's the Unborn Buddha Mind. That's what
I've been telling about just now in such detail. Weren't
you listening? [If you weren't,] it's a shame!"[89]

Blindness and the Unborn

A blind woman addressed the Master: "I have heard
that one who is physically handicapped cannot attain buddhahood. I, as you see, am blind, and without the opportunity even to worship the image of a buddha, I feel that
my being born a human has been truly in vain and that
when I die I'll just sink into the Evil Paths. If there's any
way by which even one who is blind can be said to attain
buddhahood, I beg you to instruct me."

The Master replied: "People do talk that way, but in the
Unborn I speak of, there's no distinction between being
handicapped or not being handicapped. Even if you're
blind, in the innate Buddha Mind itself there's not the
slightest difference. Do not doubt this! Just keep clear of
clinging, anger and foolishness[90] and fully affirm these
sermons I've been giving, abiding always in the Unborn
Buddha Mind, and you'll attain buddhahood right in this
life!

"There was another blind woman, in Aboshi, who asked
me the same sort of thing. When I told her what I've said
to you now, she grasped it thoroughly, and from then on
she completely changed and upheld the Unborn, telling
me time and again: 'Thanks to your instruction, I've now
gained some understanding of the fact that I am unborn.
How grateful I feel! Had I been able to see, thoughts of
clinging and craving would have been roused by whatever
I saw; I would have formed deep attachments, and how
could this faith have appeared? Strangely enough, precisely because I *was* blind, I couldn't see the good and bad
things of the world, so that such thoughts of attachment

didn't arise, and when I heard your sermon, I was able to place myself in the Unborn. It's due entirely to my blindness!'

"Thus she became a person of faith. So grasp this clearly, and your religious practice will end up going even more smoothly than that of someone who *could* see!"

When the Master had finished instructing her, this blind woman too exclaimed, "How wonderful! How marvelous!"

It is said that, convinced of the truth of the Master's words, she thoroughly acknowledged the Unborn Buddha Mind, assured beyond a doubt that even one who is handicapped can realize buddhahood.

Bodhidharma. Painted by Bankei. Property of the Ryōmonji.
(Courtesy Shunjūsha)

"The Unborn" (*fushō*). Calligraphy by Bankei. Property of the Futetsuji, Aboshi. (*Courtesy Daizō shuppan*)

Bankei's meditation rock at Nonaka in Akō, the site of his enlightenment in 1647, described in the *Sermons*. (*Courtesy Daizō shuppan*)

Portrait of Tao-che. Property of the Tafukuji, Usuki (Ōita Prefecture). (*Courtesy Daizō shuppan*)

Medicines and medicine box used by Bankei's father and elder brother. Property of the Gitoku-in, Aboshi. (*Courtesy Daizō shuppan*)

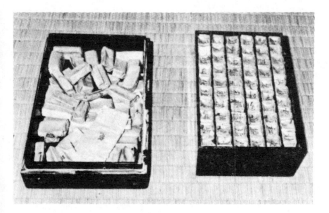

Portrait of Bankei, by the painter Yamamoto Soken (n.d.). The portrait was commissioned by Bankei's disciple Tairyō Sokyō (1638–1688). The *san*, or appreciatory verse, dated 1677, is by Bankei's colleague, the Rinzai Zen Master Kengan Zenetsu (1618–1696). (*Courtesy Shunjūsha*)

View of the Ryōmonji, showing the principal temple buildings. The Fudō
Hall stands directly to the right of the gate. To the left, are the bell (gong)
tower, the main hall and, at the far left corner, the *zendō,* or meditation
hall. (*Courtesy Daizō shuppan*)

Entry to the Ryōmonji. (*Courtesy Shunjūsha*)

Statue of Umpo, carved by Bankei. Dated 1669. Property of the Zuiōji, Akao. (*Courtesy Daizō shuppan*)

Statuette of Śākyamuni, carved by Bankei. Property of the Ryōmonji. (*Courtesy Shunjūsha*)

Returning from the bath: street scene from Bankei's period. A seventeenth century wood-block print reproduced in the *Kottōshū* (*Compendium of Curios*), an illustrated miscellany of popular manners and customs in the Tokugawa period, composed by the ukiyo-e artist and pulp writer Santō Kyōden (1716–1816).

Calligraphy by Bankei. *left:* "Transcend the buddhas, transcend the patriarchs." *center:* "*Ka!*" (a shout, the cry of enlightenment). *right:* "The pine is straight, the brambles bent." Property of the Ryōmonji. (*Courtesy Shunjūsha*)

Main gate of the Hōshinji, Marugame. (*Courtesy Shunjūsha*)

PART II

*   *   *

Now I'm going to talk to the women

"I see we have a great many women here too at the meeting today. Women tend to anger easily and stir up delusions, even over quite trivial things. I'm going to talk to the women now, but I'm sure that what I say will be familiar to everyone. Well, then, I'll begin, so pay close attention.

"For the most part, women usually busy themselves with sewing. If any of you ladies are busy sewing a kimono, or whatever, and someone happens along—an old woman, the nursemaid or whoever it might be—you'll probably start to talk. But when this happens, your sewing doesn't get in the way and prevent you from hearing what's said. And the conversation doesn't get in the way and prevent you from sewing. Without dropping your work, you can easily hear what's said and even respond appropriately— you can sew and listen too without neglecting anything. Isn't that because the marvelously illuminating Buddha Mind is unborn, so that you can both sew and listen at the same time? On the other hand, suppose you happen to be sewing, or weaving, and the thread keeps breaking, the needle snaps, or you stitch things wrong. Whichever it is, at that moment you start to seethe with impatience and fly into a rage. Terribly foolish, isn't it? How are you going to sew or weave properly when you're getting yourself angry?

When you're in the habit of losing your temper like that, the only result is that your needle snaps all the more, your thread breaks all the more!

"If, when you got angry while you worked, things got done, while when you failed to get angry, your work fell behind, then you'd be well-advised to go ahead and get yourself angry everytime you had to do anything at all. But that's simply not the way things are! In fact, just the reverse, when you get yourself angry while doing your work, the job *doesn't* get done. On the other hand, when you don't get mad, but keep a cheerful attitude and an even disposition, your work is certain to move along. However much you insist that your work gets done when you're angry, all you're doing is changing the One Buddha Mind for a fighting demon while you work. So, it seems to me that getting angry and changing your precious Unborn Buddha Mind for a fighting demon is totally useless. By getting yourselves into a temper over worthless things, you become deluded, switching your Buddha Mind for a fighting demon, a foolish beast, a covetous hungry ghost, transmigrating through every sort of [base realm]. So I want you women to pay close attention!

"There are some of you who employ others, keeping a great many errand boys and maids. Suppose one of these servants should be careless and accidentally break some valuable household object—a tea bowl or some such thing. Even though it's hardly worth making such a fuss over, the blood rushes to your face and, flying into a rage, you attack them with unreasonable severity. No matter *how* valuable a tea bowl it is, it's not as if they'd smashed it deliberately! When something is broken accidentally, there's nothing more you can do about it. But in the meanness of your selfish desire, you rashly switch the precious Buddha Mind that you were born with for a fighting demon. Isn't this even more thoughtless than smashing a tea bowl? If you buy a tea bowl, you can always replace it. What's more, between the tea you drink from a Korean tea bowl and the tea you drink from a tea bowl made in Imari,[1] there's no particular difference so far as flavor goes: either way, you've got everything you need for drinking tea. But once you've stirred up your anger, there's no going back on *it*!

"If you've clearly grasped what's involved in this business about the tea bowl, it goes without saying that with every other matter, too, it's just the same. So it's obvious without my going into each particular case. In everything else, too, just keep from moiling things over and over in your mind, getting angry and turning into a fighting demon or a foolish beast, or turning into a hungry ghost because of your selfish desires, and that's nothing but abiding naturally in the Unborn Buddha Mind. Realize the preciousness of the Buddha Mind, and even if you don't *want* to, you'll find yourself *having* to abide in the Unborn!

"What I'm telling you about not switching your Buddha Mind for the Three Poisons[2] is extremely important, so learn it well, and do your utmost not to switch your Unborn Buddha Mind for anything else."

The old nurse from Sanuki

"Let me tell you about something in this connection. When I was giving a sermon at Marugame in Sanuki, everyone in town showed up in a huge crowd to listen. The lady of a samurai retainer came with a maidservant and her old nurse, and, after hearing my instruction, returned home. Later, this lady and her nurse came again, and this time the lady told me:

" 'Before meeting your Reverence, my nurse was continually short-tempered and willful, ready to fly into a rage at the slightest thing. But ever since she heard your instruction that day, in spite of all the time that's passed, she hasn't lost her temper once. What's more, she says only sensible things and doesn't let her mind dwell at all on useless matters. The result is that I myself have now come to feel ashamed before this old nurse. She just seems to have completely grasped your Reverence's teaching, and as I believe this to be particularly thanks to you, both she and I are truly grateful.'

"Even afterwards, when I happened to hear about her, everyone told me that she'd never again strayed into delusion. The Buddha Mind I'm speaking about is unborn and marvelously illuminating, so the person for whom everything is perfectly managed with the Unborn and for whom everything functions *through* the Unborn will open the eye that sees into men and conclusively realize that everyone is a living tathagata here today. Then, like the old nurse from Sanuki, he'll keep from being deluded any more and realize the preciousness of the Buddha Mind. It's because all of you *fail* to realize the preciousness of the Buddha Mind that you stir up delusions about everything, even the most trivial matters, and remain unenlightened beings. Just keep from creating delusions, and you'll abide in the function of the marvelously illuminating Buddha Mind."

Nothing to do with rules

"That's why, in my place, I'm always telling everyone, 'Abide in the Unborn Buddha Mind and nothing else!' Other than that, I'm not setting up any special *rules*[3] and making them practice. All the same, since everyone got together and decided to practice for [a period of] twelve sticks of incense[4] every day, I told them, 'Go ahead, do whatever you like'; so I'm letting them practice every day for [a period of] twelve sticks of incense. But the Unborn Buddha Mind isn't a matter of sticks of incense! When you abide in the Buddha Mind and don't become deluded,

then, without looking for enlightenment outside, you'll
just sit in the Buddha Mind, just stand in the Buddha
Mind, just sleep in the Buddha Mind, just get up in the
Buddha Mind—just abiding in the Buddha Mind, so that
in all your ordinary activities you function as a living buddha. There's really nothing to it.

"As for zazen, since *za* ['sitting'] is the Buddha Mind's
sitting at ease, while *zen* ['meditation'] is another name for
Buddha Mind, the Buddha Mind's sitting at ease is what's
meant by zazen. So when you're abiding in the Unborn,
all the time is zazen; zazen isn't just the time when you're
practicing formal meditation. Even when you're sitting in
meditation, if there's something you've got to do, it's quite
all right to get up and leave. So, in my group, everyone is
free to do as he likes. Just always abide at ease in the
Buddha Mind. You can't simply remain sitting from morning till night, so do walking meditation[5] for one period;
and you can't just keep on your feet, either, so sit down
and meditate for one period. You can't very well do nothing but sleep, so you get up; and you can't just keep on
talking, so I let you practice meditation. But this has nothing to do with *rules*!"

Devices

"Generally speaking, Zen teachers nowadays instruct
people by setting up rules or using devices. Believing that
without devices they can't manage, behaving as if without
them it's impossible to instruct anyone, they're unable to
teach by simply pointing things out directly. To teach people
[this way], unable to manage without devices, is 'devices Zen.'

"Others tell students pursuing this teaching that it's no
good unless they rouse a great ball of doubt[6] and succeed
in breaking through it. 'No matter what,' they tell them,

'you've got to rouse a ball of doubt!' They don't teach,
'Abide in the Unborn Buddha Mind!' [but instead] cause
people *without* any ball of doubt to saddle themselves *with*
one, making them exchange the Buddha Mind for a ball
of doubt. A mistaken business, isn't it!"

Plain speaking

"In China too you have this sort of thing. As you can
see in the records that have been brought to Japan, the
true teaching of the Unborn long ago ceased to exist there,
so that nowadays, even in China, men of the Unborn are
not to be found, and that's why no records that speak of
the Unborn Buddha Mind have come to Japan.

"When I was young and trying to uncover the Buddha
Mind, I even made a serious effort at taking part in *mondō*[7]
[using Chinese expressions]. But later on, having come to
a real understanding of things, I gave it up. Japanese are
better off asking about things in a manner that's suitable *to*
Japanese, using their ordinary language. Japanese are poor
at Chinese, so in dialogues using Chinese [terms], they
can't question [teachers] about things as thoroughly as they
might wish. When you put your questions in ordinary
Japanese, there's no matter you can't ask about. So, instead
of taking a roundabout way and knocking yourselves out
trying to pose your questions in difficult Chinese words,[8]
you're better off freely putting them in easy Japanese, without exhausting yourselves. If there's some situation in which
the Dharma won't be completely realized unless you ask
your questions using Chinese words, then it's all right to
use them. But since, after all, you can manage freely by
asking your questions in ordinary Japanese, to ask them
using difficult Chinese words is a clumsy way to go about
things. So, all of you, grasp this, and whatever matter you
take up, just deal with it smoothly by asking your questions

without constraint, availing yourselves of the freedom of ordinary language. So long as you can deal with things smoothly, there's nothing so handy as your own familiar, ordinary speech.

"The reason Japanese monks are teaching laymen inept at Chinese using Chinese words that are hard for them to understand is that they *themselves* haven't settled the matter of the Unborn Buddha Mind, and evade people's questions by using Chinese words that are hard for ordinary folk to grasp. On top of which, these [difficult expressions] are nothing but the dregs and slobber of the Chinese patriarchs!

"When I was young, I determined that somehow I'd realize the marvelously illuminating Buddha Mind, and, even then, as I traveled about here and there, knocking at the doors of various teachers, I questioned them all in ordinary language and was able to manage perfectly, making myself easily understood after all. That's how things were for me. So even though at the beginning I tried out this sort of thing, afterwards I gave it up as useless. I'm not particularly learned or erudite, so it's a lucky thing I *didn't* continue engaging in *mondō* using Chinese!"

Illness and the Buddha Mind

"With my only thought to find the Buddha Mind, I struggled fruitlessly, floundering desperately and dashing all over. But what happened was that I got myself ill and was laid up in bed for a long time, so that I've come to know a lot about sickness too. Being born into this world and having a body, we must expect to meet with illness. But when you conclusively realize the Unborn Buddha Mind, you don't distress yourself over the sufferings of illness: you clearly distinguish illness as illness, suffering as suffering. This is because the Buddha Mind, being originally unborn, has nothing to do with joy or suffering, the reason being that that which is unborn transcends thought. It's when thoughts arise that you experience suffering and joy. The Buddha Mind doesn't attach to illness, it remains in the Unborn just as it is, so it doesn't create suffering. If thoughts did arise from the place of the Unborn, there would be no way you could help creating suffering, attaching to your illness and changing the Buddha Mind. [But that's hardly the case.] Even the successive sufferings of beings in hell, so far as the suffering itself is concerned, aren't any different.

"Caught up in the suffering of attaching to your illness, you start thinking one thing and another: 'I ought to be well by now. Maybe the medicine's not right; perhaps the doctor's no good . . .' and so on. Clinging to the [hope of] recovery, you switch the Buddha Mind for anguished thoughts so that the illness besetting your mind becomes worse than the original sickness. It's as if you're chasing after something that's running away. Even as you gradually do recover your [*physical*] health, the mental sickness of chasing after [it] is gaining the upper hand. That's what's meant by attaching to things and making yourself suffer.

"All the same, if there's anyone who tells you he can undergo not only illness but every kind of suffering without feeling any pain, that fellow is a liar who still hasn't realized the marvelously illuminating dynamic function of the Buddha Mind. If there's anyone who tells you he feels absolutely no pain at all, I doubt he knows the difference between feeling pain and *not* feeling it. There's simply no such thing as not feeling pain. Since the Buddha Mind is endowed with a marvelously illuminating dynamic function, not only illness but everything there is can be clearly recognized and distinguished. That's why, when you're faced with the sufferings of illness, if you simply don't get involved with them or attach to them, there's nothing you won't be able to endure. So just go *with* the illness, and, if you're in pain, go ahead and groan! But, whether you're sick or you're not, always abide in the Unborn Buddha Mind.

"However, you ought to realize that when, in response to the sufferings of illness, you become involved with thoughts, in addition to your illness, you suffer from changing the Buddha Mind for thoughts. That which is originally *without* thought is the Unborn Buddha Mind. Failing to realize the unborn [nature] of the Buddha Mind, you suffer and exchange it for thoughts. Then, no matter how much you claim you're not feeling pain, it's just talking about your *idea* of being without pain, it's merely a notion based on thought. So you aren't free from suffering after all. The fact that such thoughts even arise shows that, having failed to realize conclusively the Buddha Mind that transcends birth and death, you're *suffering* from birth and death."

Being free in birth and death

"When it comes to the idea of being free in birth and death, people are apt to misunderstand. There are some who, beforehand, announce they're going to die in a certain number of days, while others go so far as to express their intention to die, say, next *year*, in such-and-such a month and on such-and-such a day. When the time arrives, some of them, even though they're not ill, die just as they said, while others put it off for another day, or a month, and *then* pass away. There are lots of people who consider this being free in birth and death. Not that I say this isn't so. So far as freedom goes, they're *terribly* free! But things of this sort are only a result of the strength of people's ascetic practices, and often they haven't opened the Eye of the Way.[9] Even among ordinary people, you frequently find this. While they may know [the time of their] death, they haven't yet opened the Eye of the Way, and that's why I don't accept this kind of thing. The man of the Unborn *transcends* birth and death.

"Now, I'm sure you're all wondering just what it means to transcend birth and death. That which is unborn is imperishable; and since what doesn't perish doesn't die, it transcends birth and death. So, what *I* call a man who's free in birth and death is one who dies unconcerned with birth and death. What's more, the matter of birth and death is something that's with us all day long—it doesn't mean only once in a lifetime when we confront the moment of death itself. A man who's free in birth and death is one who always remains unconcerned with birth and death, knowing that so long as we're allowed to live, we live; and when the time comes to die—even if death comes right now—we just die, [realizing] that *when* we die isn't of great importance. Such a person is also one who has conclusively realized the marvelously illuminating Unborn Buddha Mind. Talking and thinking about something like what hour of what day you're going to die is really narrow-minded, don't you think?

"Then there's the idea that 'birth and death are nirvana.'[10] This again is something bound *up* with birth and death. [Everyone knows] the realm of birth and death is no different from the realm of nirvana, doesn't he? The reason [some people have to go and spell it out like this] is that they don't realize the Buddha mind everyone has from his parents innately is here, today, perfectly managing all things with the Unborn. Wrapped up in words and letters, they search about, looking for some birth and death and nirvana outside, exchanging their Unborn Buddha Mind for notions of birth and death and nirvana, so that all day long they're functioning in the realm of birth and death and haven't even a moment's peace. Pathetic, when you think of it!

"Since the Buddha Mind is perfectly managing all things with the Unborn, it doesn't know anything about 'birth and death' or 'nirvana.' From the place of the Unborn, birth and death and nirvana too are just a lot of empty speculation. That's why even for someone who up till just the other day had been involved in [the realm of] arising and ceasing, if from today on he fully realizes his mistake, and doesn't exchange the Unborn Buddha Mind for the Three Poisons or involve himself with birth and death or nirvana, he'll abide in the Unborn Buddha Mind. Then, when the time comes for the elements that compose his physical body to disperse, he'll just let them go, and die without any attachment. This is a man for whom birth and death are nirvana, a man who is free in birth and death."

The original face

"What's called one's 'original face'[11] is also none other than the Unborn Buddha Mind. What you have from your parents innately is the Unborn Buddha Mind alone—there's nothing else you've got innately. This is an expression left behind by a master of old in his attempt to make people realize the fact that the Unborn Buddha Mind is none other than one's original face. Even what we call 'father and mother' are names of traces that have already arisen. The man who has conclusively realized the Buddha Mind abides at the *source* of father and mother, and that's why we speak of [that which exists] 'before father and mother were born.' This 'before they were born' is none other than the *Un*born; so the Buddha Mind is the same as your original face. . . ."

Entrances

"Now about the Three Refuges:[12] for buddha, we take refuge in a particular buddha of our choosing; for Dharma, we take refuge in a particular Dharma; for sangha, we take refuge in a particular sangha. All I tell people about is the Buddha Mind, and that's why I'm not necessarily limited to any particular school. Differences exist in the way schools formulate their particular doctrines and teach them to people; but the only reason teachings are established is to make people realize for themselves what it is they all intrinsically possess, the Buddha Mind they have from their parents innately. So when it comes to the establishment of various schools, as they're all entrances to the Path of Buddha Mind, we call them 'entrances to the teaching.'

"There are many of you monks gathered here from every quarter for this training period, so you probably belong to many different schools. But I'm sure that as you listen to the sermons I'm giving, there will be those who affirm what I say. There are bound to be others who won't affirm it, too, and for those of you in the assembly who don't, so long as you keep from backsliding in your faith, somewhere or other the day will certainly come when you'll understand. When that happens, I'm sure you'll remember about me, so you'd better grasp what I'm saying."

To practice is hard

"Even among those in the assembly now who acknowledge what I say, there are some who merely teach the Unborn with their mouths and don't continually abide in the Unborn, people who only know *about* the Unborn, people of merely intellectual understanding. From the standpoint of the Unborn, intellectual understanding too is empty speculation, so you can't say such a person has conclusively *realized* the Unborn. When you come right down to it, this kind of approach is worthless. Even if you teach others about the Unborn, they won't realize it. And the reason they won't is that, to start with, you *yourself* haven't left everything to the Buddha Mind's unborn and marvelously illuminating [activity]; you don't *live* by the teaching or function with the Unborn at all times and in all things—you fail to practice it yourself and only teach what you know intellectually, so there's no way others are going to acknowledge it. If you don't truly acknowledge my sermon, truly practice it, truly manifest it, but just teach others what you've grasped intellectually, they can't possibly realize it themselves. In the end, this only leads to blaspheming the Dharma. So, although people who've experienced some 'realization' will turn up from time to time, there hasn't yet been one who *acts* according to his realization in all his affairs right here and now. To understand is easy; to practice is hard."

The crow and the cormorant

"That's why, when it comes to my disciples in permanent residence at the temple, if they haven't opened the Eye of the Way, if they lack the eye that sees into men, I forbid them to teach. If they *are* teaching like this, they're only mimicking my words. As the saying goes, when a crow tries to imitate a cormorant, his black coloring may be the same, but once he's in the water, he's unable to function freely the way the cormorant does. In exactly the same way, just as the crow's black coloring is like the cormorant's, students who imitate the way I speak may be able to mouth things about the Unborn Buddha Mind. But since those whose eye hasn't opened to the marvelously illuminating [activity] of this Buddha Mind lack the eye that sees into men, when they have to respond to people's questions, somehow they find themselves tongue-tied and can't function freely. It's the same as the crow when he gets in the water and can't function freely the way the cormorant does. That's why I strictly forbid my disciples to teach. It's because, without knowing the Unborn, people just stay on the plane of understanding, of what's seen or heard, felt or thought,[13] and exchange the Buddha Mind for notions. This is what's meant by delusion."

Let it be

"The reason people misunderstand the difference between thoughts and delusions is that everyone imagines thoughts all exist at the bottom and arise from there; but originally there's no actual substance at the 'bottom' from which thoughts arise. Instead, you retain the things you see and hear, and from time to time, in response to circumstances, the impressions created by these experiences are reflected back to you in precise detail. So when they're reflected, just let them be, and refrain from attaching to them. Even if *evil* thoughts come up, just let them come up, don't involve yourself with them, and they can't help but stop. Isn't this just the same as if they didn't arise? That way, there won't be any evil thoughts for you to drive out forcefully, or any remorse about having had them.

"Because the Buddha Mind is marvelously illuminating, mental impressions from the past are reflected, and you make the mistake of labeling as 'delusions' things that aren't delusions at all. Delusions means the anguish of thought feeding on thought. What foolishness it is to create the anguish of delusion by changing the precious Buddha Mind, pondering over this and that, mulling over things of no worth! If there were anyone who actually succeeded at something by pondering it all the way through, it might be all right to do things that way; but *I've* never heard of anyone who, in the end, was able to accomplish anything like this! So, pondering over things is useless, isn't it? It's utterly useless! The main thing is always to be careful not to stir up thoughts and change the Unborn Buddha Mind for a fighting demon, a hell-dweller, a hungry ghost, a beast, and the like. If you do, you won't have another chance to be born a human, not in ten thousand or even one *hundred* thousand kalpas!"

The lawsuit

"Luckily, I happen to recall something in this connection, so let me tell you all about it. I've got a temple, the Fumonji,[14] at Hirado in Hizen province. Last year, when I was giving sermons at this temple, the people from three or four *ri*[15] around came to listen, and we had as big a crowd as the one that comes to the Nyohōji[16] in Ōzu in Iyo. [At this time,] there were two merchants from Hirado, an uncle and nephew, who were embroiled in a lawsuit. The uncle had filed a formal petition of complaint with the magistrate and was pressing it determinedly, but, whatever the nature of the suit, it proved a difficult one, and even the magistrate was hard put to resolve it and had become fed up with the whole affair. For three years the case dragged on, bitterly deadlocked. Meanwhile, having failed to reach any settlement, the uncle and nephew stopped exchanging visits and broke off all relations.

"Then, one day, the uncle came to hear my sermon, and gradually became convinced by what he heard.

"'Truly,' he considered, 'up till now I'd never dreamed I was exchanging the Buddha Mind I have from my parents innately for a fighting demon, a hell-dweller, a beast or a hungry ghost! I'm sure there's no greater unfiliality toward one's parents! What's more, a nephew is an intimate member of the family, just like one's own son—it's not as if he were a stranger. Yet, the truth is that, because of the baseness of my own desires, I've been indulging in self-centeredness, which isn't at *all* innate, attached to worldly concerns. How could I ever let things come to this—uncle and nephew turned into mortal enemies, about to condemn themselves to transmigrate forever, dying and being reborn amid the Three Evil Realms!' Reflecting like this, without even returning home, he went straight from where I was giving the sermon to see the magistrate and told him: 'I have put your Honor to much trouble in this lawsuit with my nephew and am sincerely grateful for all you've done. However, today for the first time I heard the Venerable Bankei's sermon, and I've realized my mistake. Misled by my own petty desires, with no shame about what people might say, I brought charges against my own nephew before your Honor, pressing them relentlessly, filled only with hatred and lacking any sympathy at all. Now that I've realized my error, I feel completely ashamed. Hearing the Venerable Bankei's instruction, I was truly saved, so from here on I'm abandoning my lawsuit. I therefore humbly request your Honor to return to me the petition I gave you.'

"The magistrate readily agreed, and, filled with admiration, declared: 'Truly, his Reverence's superior virtue is not limited only to Buddhism but is able to manage worldly affairs and government as well! On your part, too, how extraordinary that you acknowledged his teaching, forgiving your nephew and abandoning the lawsuit.' With these words of praise, he handed back the petition.

"The uncle, having received the petition from the magistrate, first returned to his home, and then, placing the petition inside his robe, [went off to see] the nephew whom he hadn't visited for three years.

"Since the uncle had come entirely on his own, putting

aside his stubborn willfulness, he took the nephew completely by surprise.

" 'Strange,' he thought to himself, dumbfounded: 'This uncle files a lawsuit against me for three years, severs all contact between us, doesn't pay a single visit, and now he comes to see me this way! Why? It certainly is hard to figure. What's going on? It just doesn't feel right.'

"Still, there was his uncle, and, even while they might not have been on speaking terms, now that he had arrived and announced himself, there was no way the nephew could escape, so he told him: 'Welcome. Please come in.' And while the nephew was thinking: 'I wonder what he's got to say?' his uncle declared:

" 'I realize my coming here must seem strange, but I had to tell you this: You and I are uncle and nephew, but, old as I am, I've acted like a child, setting myself against you who are young, wrongfully starting a lawsuit and breaking off all relations between us for three years. But today, after hearing the Venerable Bankei's wonderful teaching, I'm completely ashamed of myself. I've behaved disgracefully in front of everyone, and now, filled with remorse, I've come here to offer my apologies, so please forgive me for the wrong I've done. And to prove to you that I'm not going to prosecute this lawsuit any further, today, as soon as I left the place where the Venerable Bankei was delivering his talk, I went straight to the magistrate, took back the petition I'd given him, and brought it here to show to you and set your mind at ease. Here, see for yourself!' the uncle said, drawing the lawsuit from his robe.

"Thinking, 'Well, I'd never expected him to behave like such a model uncle!' the nephew said: 'What could be more wonderful! I was at fault for failing to accord you the respect due as my senior. I've truly violated Heaven's will and feel completely ashamed. I have no parents now, so, whatever it was, it was my duty to ask your advice and

accept your orders and instructions. Instead, my behavior
has been unmentionable. Whatever you told me, it was
my duty to obey you, without any protest, but I opposed
you and drove you to file a lawsuit with the magistrate. To
have acted like this was unmindful of the Way of Heaven,
heedless of the gods and buddhas. There is nowhere I can
hide my shame before my own dead father. Please forgive
me! I quarreled and broke off relations with you, my re-
spected uncle, and then, "once the ship was under way,
there was no turning back," no choice except to stop seeing
one another till now. If the truth be told, it was for me to
come to you and present *my* apologies. The fact that, in
the end, it was you, my uncle, who came *here* and spoke
to me like this shows the most shameless behavior on my
part. How grateful I feel!' So saying, he poured forth tears
and declared: 'In all our quarrels before, the fault was
entirely my own, uncle, so I beg you to forgive me!'

"When the nephew had spoken, the uncle said: 'No,
no! Not at all! The fault is mine, and it's *I* who ask for
forgiveness. When one is young, as you were, it's common, whoever it is, to act rashly, not knowing what's good
or bad, right or wrong in the world, not caring what others
may think. But even though you weren't grown, I turned
against you, believing you were a detestable character—
and you too, in your turn, must have become convinced
that *I* was behaving heartlessly, so that both of us nearly
condemned ourselves to transmigrate forever, with no hope
of escape, sunk in an eternity of accumulated sin! How
ashamed I feel now when I think of it!'

"They didn't stop at merely ending the lawsuit, but
with each of them insisting like this on taking all the blame,
they patched up their three years' breach. The uncle lin-
gered leisurely at the nephew's house and was lavishly feasted
before returning home; and later, the nephew put on his
formal attire and returned the courtesy by going to visit his
uncle. The result was that, after this, they became even

closer to one another than they had been before the lawsuit. This sort of thing can really happen!

"All who witnessed the sincere relationship between the uncle and nephew were amazed and deeply moved. Those in the neighboring towns who were conducting lawsuits of their own, on hearing about this, yielded to reason, gave way in their selfish insistence and went each and every one to withdraw the lawsuits they'd presented. Some seventeen petitions had been submitted to the magistrates, but, nevertheless, I understand that all seventeen were withdrawn. In fact, as someone from Hirado told me, this uncle had always been a thoroughly hard-nosed character—not at all the sort you'd expect to go to the *nephew*! But those who are hard-nosed will also give way easily.

"Considering the whole matter of this lawsuit between the uncle and nephew, don't you think it's pathetic the way they became deluded as a result of their shameless selfishness toward one another and the strength of their self-centeredness, not even realizing that others were regarding them with scorn and speaking badly of them, making them the object of all kinds of talk? Of course, when it's someone else's suits and litigations, you can talk glibly about the rights and wrongs; but when *you're* the one concerned, it's not so easy! Because of selfish desire, to rationalize your own position just to get what you want, acting willfully and wrongfully, changing the precious Buddha Mind for desire and falling into the realm of hungry ghosts, obscuring the marvelously illuminating Buddha Mind and becoming a beast—this is the greatest unfiliality you can show your parents.

"I'm telling you people this sort of thing in the hope it will prove instructive to all of you too. The uncle's having instantly given way and been saved when he heard a single sermon was also entirely due to the dynamic function you intrinsically possess, the precious Buddha Mind you have from your parents innately!"

*   *   *

Mu

A monk who had gone to see the Master in private interview said: "I received the koan 'Jōshū's Mu'[17] from a certain Zen teacher and worked at it for many years, applying myself single-mindedly, exerting all my strength, never leaving it from my mind even when moving my hands or feet; but, try as I did, I couldn't solve it. What's more, even though I drove myself so hard that afterward I was ill for quite some time, nothing special happened. In fact, on the contrary, I became a sick man, and, after a whole year of being exhausted by illness, gave up my work on the Mu koan. When I simply kept my mind like the empty sky, I felt remarkably easy in both mind and body, and gradually recovered my health. Today, then, I'm no longer working on the Mu koan, and, while I don't feel I've solved it, since I always keep my mind like the empty sky, I'm quite content. Still, I'd very much like to receive your instruction."

The Master replied: "To put aside the koan Mu and keep your mind like the empty sky isn't bad since it's [at least] an expression of your own spiritual power. But, while it's all right, it's hardly the ultimate. Since your Unborn Buddha Mind hasn't been realized, you can't manage smoothly in your actual daily affairs. In exchanging it for something like 'the empty sky,' you're obscuring the marvelously illuminating Buddha Mind, and the result is, you lack the eye that sees into men. Unless you open the eye that sees into men, you're a blind man and won't be able to see into others. How about it? I'm sure the minds of others must be quite invisible to you."

The monk said: "Yes, it's true."

The Master told him: "It's only natural! So do as I say,

thoroughly affirm what I'm telling you. When you accept what you've heard and conclusively realize it, then and there the eye that sees into men will appear, and you won't make any mistake about things. That moment is the complete realization of the Dharma."

The crows go kaa-kaa, the sparrows, chuu-chuu

The Master addressed the assembly: "Just as always, every single day when I come out to talk, today too the crows go *kaa-kaa*, the sparrows, *chuu-chuu*, and I haven't anything different to say myself. All the same, when you really acknowledge this one word ['unborn'],[18] you'll find everything is smoothly managed.

"The proof of this is that, while all of you here are turned toward me, intent only on hearing my sermon and wondering, 'What's Bankei going to say?' you aren't trying either to hear or not to hear the cawing of the crows and the chirping of the sparrows out in back. But, even so, once they start to chirp and caw, you recognize and distinguish the crow's *kaa-kaa* and the sparrow's *chuu-chuu*. And it's not only for crows and sparrows: everything here, when you perceive it with the Unborn, will be simultaneously distinguished, and you won't overlook even one thing in one hundred or one thousand. In the meanwhile, if a gong rings outside the temple, you know it's a gong, if a drum sounds, you know it's a drum. Your distinguishing everything you see and hear like this, without producing a single thought, is the marvelously illuminating dynamic function, the Buddha Mind that is unborn."

Two-thirds is with the Unborn

"If you divided the day into three parts, you'd find that, of all your activities from morning till night, two-thirds would be managed with the Unborn. Yet, without realizing this, you imagine you operate entirely through cleverness and discrimination—a serious error indeed! As for the remaining third, unable to abide in the Unborn, you change your Buddha Mind for thoughts, attaching to things that come your way, so that even right in this life you're creating fighting demons, creating beasts, creating hungry ghosts, and when your life comes to a close, you fall right into the Three Evil Realms. To believe the Three Evil Realms exist *after* you die is a great mistake, a bit of far-fetched speculation!"

Looking for enlightenment

"To exert yourselves in religious practice, trying to produce enlightenment by doing religious practices and zazen, is all wrong too. There's no difference between the mind of all the buddhas and the Buddha Mind of each one of you. But by wanting to realize enlightenment, you create a duality between the one who *realizes* enlightenment and what it is that's being realized. When you cherish even the smallest desire to realize enlightenment, right away you leave behind the realm of the Unborn and go against the Buddha Mind. This Buddha Mind you have from your parents innately is one alone—not two, not three!"

*   *   *

No delusion, no enlightenment

"You people all imagine you'd become buddhas now for the first time. But the Buddha Mind you have from your parents innately is unborn, so it has no beginning and no end. There's not even a hair's breadth of anything you can call delusion. So get it squarely in your minds that there's nothing arising from inside. The main thing is simply not getting involved with the world of externals.[19] That which isn't involved with the world of externals is the Buddha Mind, and since the Buddha Mind is marvelously illuminating, when you abide in this marvelously illuminating Buddha Mind just as it is, there's no delusion, no enlightenment. Whether you're making a fist or running about, it's all the unborn functioning of the Buddha Mind. What's more, if you're the least bit in a rush to become a superior person right away, you'll immediately go counter to the Unborn and leave it far behind. In the innate Buddha Mind, there's neither joy, sorrow nor anger—nothing but the Buddha Mind itself, marvelously illuminating and distinguishing [all things].

"So, when you distinguish the things that confront you in the world of externals—joy, sorrow, anger, or anything under the sun—it's the dynamic function of the marvelously illuminating Buddha Mind, the Buddha Mind you originally possess."

*　　*　　*

Water and ice

"Since the Buddha Mind each of you has innately isn't 'created,' it doesn't contain even a speck of delusion. So anyone who says, 'I'm deluded because I'm an unenlightened being' is a terribly unfilial person slandering his own parents! In the Buddha Mind you have from your parents innately, the buddhas of the past and the people of the present are all one substance, with no difference between them. It's just like the water of the ocean: In the depths of winter, the water freezes and turns to ice, assuming various forms—angular, or round; but when it melts, it's all the one water of the ocean. When you realize the unborn nature of the Buddha Mind, that's the water *itself*, just as it is, and you can freely dip your hands right in!"[20]

Stopping thoughts

"Since the Unborn Buddha Mind is marvelously illuminating, it hasn't so much as a hair's breadth of any selfish bias, so it adapts itself freely, and, as it encounters different sorts of circumstances, thoughts sporadically pop up. It's all right so long as you simply don't get involved with them; but if you do get involved with thoughts and go on developing them, you won't be able to stop, and then you'll obscure the marvelously illuminating [function] of the Buddha Mind and create delusions. On the other hand, since from the start the Buddha Mind is marvelously illuminating, readily illumining and distinguishing all things, when you hate and loathe those deluded thoughts that come up and try to *stop* them, you get caught up in stopping them and create a duality between the one who is doing the stopping and that which is being stopped. If you try to stop thought with thought, there will never be an end to it. It's just like trying to wash away blood with blood. Even if you succeed in getting out the original blood, you'll be left with the stain of the blood that came after."

*   *   *

The mirror

"Since this Buddha Mind is unborn and marvelously illuminating, it's a thousand, ten thousand times brighter than a mirror, and there's nothing it doesn't recognize and distinguish. With a mirror, no sooner do the forms of things pass before it, than their reflected images appear.

Because, from the start, the mirror is without conscious intention, it hasn't any thought of rejecting or not rejecting the forms of things that come before it, no thought to remove or not to remove those images it reflects. This is the function of the shining mirror. We can't help comparing the marvelously illuminating function of the Buddha Mind to a mirror, so I'm simply making the comparison. But the mirror doesn't even come close—the Buddha Mind is a thousand times, *ten* thousand times more wonderful!

"With the dynamic function of the marvelously illuminating Buddha Mind, every object that comes before your eyes is individually recognized and distinguished without your doing a thing. So, even though you're not *trying* to do so, you recognize thousands of different impressions by sight or by sound. All these are things with form, but even those *without* form—the things in people's hearts that can't be seen—are precisely reflected. Even with the different sorts of faces you encounter, their good or evil thoughts are reflected by the marvelously illuminating Buddha Mind.

"Take the people assembled here, intent on listening to my talk: If someone happens to cough, you're not making a deliberate effort to listen; but as soon as there's coughing—even though you're not trying either to hear it or not to hear it—you can distinguish it well enough to say whether that cough just now came from a man or a woman, an old person or a young one. Or take the case of someone whom you last saw twenty years before: You haven't seen him since, and then, by chance, you meet on the street and, prompted by this encounter, the events of twenty years before at once spring clearly to mind. How different this is from the function of the mirror!"

Fire is hot

"This sort of thing, your recognizing and distinguishing instantly and spontaneously whatever you see and hear, is the dynamic function of the Buddha Mind you have from your parents innately, the Buddha Mind, unborn and marvelously illuminating.

"As another example of the unborn function of the Buddha Mind: When you're just there with no particular thought at all and someone puts a flame to your fingertips, you give a start, and, without thinking, automatically pull back your hand. This too is proof that the marvelously illuminating Buddha Mind is unborn and perfectly manages [everything]. On the other hand, to think, 'That was a flame just now,' and then realize, 'It's hot!' and get angry with the fellow who burned you is to fall into the realm of secondary experience, deliberating after the fact."

* * *

Be stupid!

"I tell my students and those of you coming regularly here to the temple: 'Be stupid!' Because you've got the dynamic function of the marvelously illuminating Buddha Mind, even if you get rid of discriminative understanding, you won't be foolish. So, all of you, from here on, be stupid! Even if you're stupid, when you're hungry, you'll ask for something to eat, when you're thirsty, you'll ask for some tea; when it gets warm, you'll put on thin, light clothes, and when it's cold, you'll put on more clothes. As far as your activities of today are concerned, you're not lacking a thing![21]

"With people who are clever, there are sure to be a great many shortcomings. To have transcended those clever people whom all the world holds in great esteem is what's meant by 'stupidity.' There's really nothing wrong with being a blockhead!

"When people say that someone is a clever fellow, I ask

to meet him, and when I do and we have a chance to talk, it looks to me as if people in the world are praising an awful lot of foolishness. The fact is that those clever people acclaimed by the world are, from the start, deluded by their own cleverness. They distort the Buddha Mind and obscure its marvelously illuminating [dynamic function], considering other people as of no account, contradicting whatever they say, slighting and insulting them. Of course, since those they're insulting are *also* amply endowed with the marvelously illuminating Buddha Mind, they aren't going to let themselves be slighted like that, so they get angry and answer right back, heedlessly pouring forth abuse. The *true* man's ideal is to show kindness to those who are foolish and help those who are evil. To be recognized as a good man by the people of the world is precisely what makes being born a human being worthwhile. How can it be any good to earn yourself the reputation of a wicked person?

"So when you go back to your homes and meet your old acquaintances, you should have them wondering about you all: 'How did Bankei teach them Buddhism, anyway? Why, they've come back even more stupid than before they left!'

"What I'm talking about isn't the stupidity of stupidity and understanding. That which *transcends* stupidity and understanding is what *I* mean by stupidity!"

Smoking

"I know it's something I'm telling you day after day, but don't get into bad habits! Bad habits occur when you attach to things that others do. These things become ingrained so that you can't get them out of your mind, and end up by forming bad habits.

"Take smoking: Is there anyone who's a smoker right

from birth? No, indeed! Seeing others smoke, you imitate them, and then your smoking becomes ingrained and turns into a bad habit. Even when you're in the presence of important persons, or in places where smoking isn't allowed, you still have the urge to smoke, and all because you've got into the bad habit of being accustomed to smoke all the time. What's more, when you're thirsty and you smoke tobacco, it doesn't quench your thirst; and when you're starving, I've never heard that you could satisfy your *hunger* by smoking, either! Yet, despite the fact that it's a completely worthless activity, once you happen to pick up smoking and make it a habit, it becomes something you just can't stop. Through this one example, you can clearly understand every situation. So, even in small things, avoid creating bad habits and making yourself deluded."

*   *   *

No such thing as enlightenment

A monk who had come from Sendai in Ōshū[22] said: "Somewhere I seem to recall there being the expression, 'The mind enslaved to physical form.'[23] I'm anxious to accord with original mind at all times, but how should I practice in order to do this? Please instruct me."

The Master replied: "In my school, there's no special form of instruction; and as for religious practice, there's no particular way for doing that either. People fail to realize that right within themselves they're fully endowed with the Buddha Mind they have from their parents innately, so they lose their freedom and talk about wanting to 'accord with original mind.' When you've realized that the Buddha Mind you have from your parents is unborn and marvelously illuminating, your hands and feet will function freely, and that's the working of the marvelously illuminating Buddha Mind which is unborn.

"As proof that your Buddha Mind is unborn and freely functioning: When you came from Sendai having heard about Bankei, you traveled a long way; but as you stopped for the night here and there along the road, you weren't thinking continuously about me. In the daytime, you looked around at all the sights, and if you had traveling companions, you talked to them. But even though you didn't walk along thinking about our meeting and deliberately keeping it in mind at every step of the way, in the end you arrived here at my place. This is what's meant by the Buddha Mind being unborn and perfectly managing things.

"Now, the herons you see in Sendai are white, without having to be dyed that way; and the crows, without being dyed, are black. And right here too, even though when you see them you're not deliberately trying to distinguish between the two, as soon as they appear before you, you know the white one's a heron and the black one's a crow. Without rousing a single thought, it's all smoothly managed, isn't it? . . . ."

Then, the monk asked: "I find it impossible to control all my passions and delusions. What should I do? It's simply proved too much for me, and I wish to receive your instruction."

The Master replied: "Your idea of wanting to control your passions and delusions is *itself* delusion, changing the Buddha Mind for delusion! Delusions don't have any actual substance when they arise. In fact, they're nothing but shadow figures, things you've seen and heard that pop up sporadically in response to circumstances."

Again, the monk questioned the Master: "What is enlightenment?"

The Master replied: "There's no such thing as enlightenment. It's a completely extraneous pursuit. To realize conclusively that the Buddha Mind you have from your parents innately is unborn and marvelously illuminating—*that's* enlightenment. *Not* realizing this makes you deluded. Since the Original Buddha Mind is unborn, it functions without thoughts of delusion or thoughts of wanting to be enlightened. As soon as you think of wanting to be enlightened, you leave the place of the Unborn and go counter to it. Because the Buddha Mind is unborn, it has no thoughts at all. Thoughts are the source of delusion. When thoughts are gone, delusion vanishes too. And once you've stopped being deluded, talking about wanting to attain 'enlightenment' certainly is useless, don't you agree?"

Abide in the Buddha Mind

A monk asked: "My regular practice is to read the sutras and perform zazen. I feel these activities are meritorious and do them all the time. Should I now give them up as useless?"

The Master replied: "Practicing zazen and reading the sutras is fine. Zazen is something that all monks who seek to draw the water of Shaka's stream must practice and not despise. Daruma's wall-gazing,[24] Tokusan's ridding himself of his sutras,[25] Gutei's raising his finger,[26] Rinzai's '*katsu!*'[27]— even though these vary according to the different circumstances at the time and the particular manner of the teacher involved, they all just have to do with experiencing for yourself the One Unborn Buddha Mind. You don't mistake the sound of a gong for that of a drum, the sound of a crow for that of a sparrow, the sound of a sparrow for that of a crow—all the sounds you hear are individually recognized and distinguished without your missing a single one. It's the marvelously illuminating Buddha Mind that's listening, the Buddha Mind which is unborn. The words of Rinzai's Record[28] and these things I'm telling you are exactly the same, there's no difference between them. From here, the only question is whether or not you have faith.

If you can't abide in the Unborn Buddha Mind just as it is, and stir up different thoughts, regretting the past, worrying about the future, then, in just a day's time, without even knowing it, turning and transforming, you'll have changed the Buddha Mind for passing thoughts, and you'll never have a moment's peace!

"Now, you may be doing zazen and reading the sutras, but abide in the Buddha Mind that you have from your parents innately, just as it is, and realize the Unborn. If you practice zazen or read the sutras with some deliberate aim in mind, hoping to accumulate merit, or whatever, you'll only be changing the Buddha Mind for merit, or changing it for zazen and sutras! That's how it is, so all you've got to do is acknowledge with profound faith and realization that, without *your* producing a single thought or resorting to any cleverness or shrewdness, everything is individually recognized and distinguished of itself. And all because the marvelously illuminating Buddha Mind is unborn and smoothly manages each and every thing."

When thoughts arise

A novice of fourteen or fifteen asked: "When I practice zazen, thoughts seem to come up. What should I do about this?"

The Master replied: "To distinguish and recognize each one of the different thoughts that arise—that's none other than the dynamic function of the Buddha Mind. Because the Buddha Mind is unborn and marvelously illuminating as well, whatever things are retained in your mind rise to the surface. In the Buddha Mind, there *aren't* any thoughts or 'things'; so when you don't get yourself involved with them, don't worry about trying to get rid of them or stop them, you'll just naturally accord with the Unborn Buddha Mind."

*　　*　　*

Letting things take care of themselves

The Master instructed a monk who had come from Tamba:[29] "To take the attitude that, having come all this way, you want to be sure and realize buddhahood now as quickly as you can is to be deluded by your consuming desire for buddhahood. This may seem like something perfectly fine and admirable, but it is, in fact, deluded. When it comes to me, I never even quote the words of the buddhas and patriarchs in the sutras and records. And if you want to know why, it's because I can manage perfectly dealing with people's own selves, so that's all I talk to them about.

"Your wanting to realize buddhahood as quickly as you can is useless to begin with. Since the Buddha Mind you have from your parents is unborn and marvelously illuminating, before even a single thought is produced, all things are recognized and distinguished without resorting to any cleverness. Without attaching to [notions of] 'enlightened' or 'deluded,' just remain in the state where all things are recognized and distinguished. Let things take care of themselves, and whatever comes along will be smoothly managed—whether you like it or not! That's the [working of the] Buddha Mind and its marvelously illuminating dynamic function. Like a mirror that's been perfectly polished, without producing a single thought, with no awareness on your part, without even realizing it, each and every thing is smoothly dealt with as it comes from outside. Not understanding this, you people take all the credit and act as if you managed everything yourselves by means of cleverness! That's why you can't help remaining deluded. If you clearly grasp that thought is something you produce yourself when you get involved with things that come along, and keep from switching [the Buddha Mind] for some 'thing,' why, that's the basis of religious practice; and it's also what's meant when we say that the Buddha Mind is unborn, our own intrinsic and marvelously illuminating dynamic function."

HŌGO (Instruction)

Duality

A layman asked: "I'm grateful for your teaching of the Unborn, but I find that thoughts easily come up as a result of my ingrained bad habits, and when I'm distracted by them, I can't wholeheartedly realize the Unborn. How can I put my faith totally [in the Unborn Buddha Mind]?"

The Master said: "When you try to stop your rising thoughts, you create a duality between the mind that does the stopping and the mind that's being stopped, so you'll never have peace of mind. Just have faith that thoughts don't originally exist, but only arise and cease temporarily in response to what you see and hear, without any actual substance of their own."

(*zenshū*, p. 124.)

The dog and the chicken

A layman asked: "I have heard that thoughts of foolishness and ignorance lead to becoming a beast, so that one goes from darkness into darkness, unable to realize buddhahood. However, when a beast has no awareness it's pathetic, it fails to realize that being the way it is is agony, so can't it, after all, be perfectly content?"

The Master replied: "Isn't it lamentable to transform

the Buddha Mind and Buddha Body everyone has innately into the agony of a hell-dweller, not even realizing how pathetic this is! For example, when you drive off and abuse the dog who stole your chicken the day before, the dog doesn't realize it's because he stole the chicken, so when he meets with this abuse, he barks and howls in anguish. Being an animal, he can't understand the law of cause and effect and has to go on suffering endlessly. Because human beings are endowed with bright wisdom, when they have the chance to meet a wise teacher they can readily attain buddhahood. A wonderful thing, isn't it, having the good fortune to be born in a human body in which you may easily realize buddhahood? Just such a great matter stands right before your eyes. Don't fritter away your time!"

(zenshū, p. 125.)

*   *   *

Farming with the Buddha Mind

A farmer asked: "I'm short-tempered by nature and easily get angry. Because I'm a farmer, I'm wholly taken up with my chores and it's hard for me to realize the Unborn. How can I be in accord with the Unborn Mind?"

The Master said: "Everyone has the Unborn Buddha Mind innately, so there's no way you're going to be in accord with it now for the first time! To perform your work as a farmer single-mindedly is practicing the Unborn Mind. When you're at work with your hoe, you may be speaking with someone at the same time, but even if you're absorbed in the conversation, it doesn't interfere with your hoeing; and if you're absorbed in hoeing, it doesn't interfere with your carrying on a conversation. Even when you're angry, you can still go on hoeing, but since anger is the evil cause of becoming a hell-dweller, [your work] turns into a difficult and painful practice. When you do your hoeing without delusions like anger, [your work] will become an easy and joyful practice. This is the practice of the Buddha Mind, the practice of the Unborn and Imperishable."

(*zenshū*, pp. 125–126.)

The travelers

A monk asked: "I have heard that the masters of old reached great enlightenment through difficult and painful practice, and that it was through various sorts of difficult practice that the masters of our own day too attained complete realization of the Dharma. I can't quite accept the idea that someone like myself can realize the Unborn Buddha Mind just as I am without engaging in religious practice or attaining enlightenment."

The Master said: "Suppose there's a group of travelers passing through tall mountain peaks. Arriving at a spot where there's no water, they become thirsty, and one of them goes off to search for water in a distant valley. After strenuously searching all over, he finds some at last and returns to give it to his companions to drink. Without making any strenuous efforts themselves, the people who drink the water can satisfy their thirst just the same as the one who did make such efforts, can't they? [On the other hand,] those who harbor doubts and refuse to drink the water will have no way to satisfy their thirst. Because I didn't meet with any clear-eyed men, I went astray and engaged in strenuous efforts till finally I uncovered the buddha within my own mind. So when I tell all of you that, without painful practice, you [can uncover] the buddha in your own minds, it's just like [the travelers] drinking the water and slaking their thirst without having gone in search of the water themselves. In this way, when you make use of the Buddha Mind that everyone has, just as it is, and attain peace of mind without delusory difficult practice, that's the precious true teaching, isn't it?"

(*zenshū*, p. 126.)

* * *

Parents

A nun from Izumo asked: "Both my parents are still living. How should I observe my filial duty toward them?"

The Master replied: "There's no particular manner in which one must express filiality. Simply abiding in the Buddha Mind you have from your parents innately, just as it is—this is the true practice of filiality. Failing to do this is what it means to be *un*filial."

(*zenshū*, pp. 126–127.)

Becoming an expert at delusion

The Master addressed the assembly: "Originally, at birth, you were all without any sort of delusion. But, because of your bad upbringing, you turned the innate Buddha Mind into a first-rate unenlightened being, imitating and taking on all the delusions you saw around you and forming bad habits, so that you ended up becoming regular experts at delusion! It's because the Buddha Mind is marvelously [functioning] that you pick up all sorts of deluded [behavior] that then become second nature to you. Nevertheless, when, hearing about this sort of precious thing,[1] you rouse your faith and resolve to keep from being deluded, right then and there you'll abide in the original Unborn, just as it is. So, it's because the Buddha Mind is marvelously illuminating that you're deluded; and it's also because the

Buddha Mind is marvelously illuminating that you're *enlightened*. Since you don't realize the preciousness of the Buddha Mind, you think the delusions that are harming you are treasures of great value. And you value these *so* highly, that you become deluded and throw your life away! Isn't that thoughtless? Isn't it foolish?"

(*zenshū*, p. 127.)

The living Buddha Mind

The Master addressed the assembly: "For one who at all times conclusively realizes the Buddha Mind, when he goes to bed, he goes to bed with the Buddha Mind; when he gets up, he gets up with the Buddha Mind; when he stays, he stays with the Buddha Mind; when he goes, he goes with the Buddha Mind; when he sits, he sits with the Buddha Mind; when he stands, he stands with the Buddha Mind; when he sleeps, he sleeps with the Buddha Mind; when he wakes up, he wakes up with the Buddha Mind; when he speaks, he speaks with the Buddha Mind; when he's silent, he's silent with the Buddha Mind; when he eats rice, he eats with the Buddha Mind; when he drinks tea, he drinks with the Buddha Mind; when he puts on his clothes, he puts them on with the Buddha Mind. At all times he abides continually in the Buddha Mind, and there's not a single moment when he *isn't* in the Buddha Mind. He functions with perfect freedom in accordance with circumstances, letting things take their way. Just do good things and don't do bad ones. If you pride yourself on [your] good deeds, however, becoming attached to them and abominating the bad, that's going against the Buddha Mind. The Buddha Mind is neither good *nor* bad, but operates beyond them both. Isn't that the living Buddha Mind? When you've conclusively realized this and haven't any doubts, then and there you'll open the eye that penetrates men's minds. That's why my school is called the Clear-Eyed School."

(zenshū, p. 127.)

The "teetotaler"

A layman asked: "I don't doubt that, originally, deluded thoughts don't exist; but since the flow of my thoughts never stops for even a moment, it's impossible for me to realize the Unborn."

The Master said: "When you came into this world, there was only the Unborn Buddha Mind. As you grew, however, you picked up the ignorant attitudes you saw around you, so that, as time passed, you got *used* to being deluded, and the deluded mind gained a free hand. Originally, in your innate self, thoughts don't exist, so in the mind that affirms and has faith in its own unborn buddhahood, thoughts simply vanish. It's like a man who's fond of wine but gets sick from it and has to stop drinking. If he finds himself in a situation where wine is served, thoughts of wanting to drink may arise, but since he *doesn't* drink, he neither gets sick nor drunk. He's a 'teetotaler' even while thoughts of drinking arise, and ends up a healthy man. Delusory thoughts are like this too. When you simply let them arise or cease, without either taking them up or rejecting them, then, before you know it, they'll vanish in the Mind of the Unborn."

(zenshū, pp. 127–128.)

Suppression is delusion too

A monk asked: "I find it impossible to suppress all my defilements and delusions. What can I do to suppress them?"

The Master replied: "Trying to suppress delusion is delusion too. Delusions have no original existence; they're only things you create yourself by indulging in discrimination."

(zenshū, p. 128.)

Right now

A visiting monk asked: "In your sermon the other evening, you stated that everyone innately possesses the Buddha Mind. While I'm grateful for your instruction, it seems to me that if everyone were endowed with the Buddha Mind, deluded thoughts couldn't arise."

The Master replied: "Right now as you're saying this, what delusions *are* there?"

The monk prostrated himself three times and withdrew.

(zenshū, p. 128.)

Sleeping and waking

A layman asked: "I admit that we see and hear with the Unborn. But when we fall asleep, we're unaware even of another person right beside us, so at that time we seem to lose the vital function of the Unborn."

The Master said: "What kind of loss is there? There's no loss at all. You've simply fallen asleep."

(zenshū, p. 128.)

*　　*　　*

Sendai

A monk from Sendai[2] came and asked: "How can I realize original mind?"

The Master answered: "Apart from the one who's asking me at this moment, there *is* no original mind. This original mind transcends thought, clearly distinguishing all things. And isn't the proof of this that when I ask you about anything to do with Sendai, you're able to answer without the slightest reflection?"

(*zenshū*, p. 129.)

The place of the Unborn

A visiting monk asked: "If one truly realizes the Unborn, after the four elements of the physical body[3] have dispersed, will he be born again or not?"

The Master replied: "In the place of the Unborn, the whole question of being born or not being born is irrelevant."

(*zenshū*, p. 129.)

Letting go

A layman said: "Some years ago, I asked you what I should do to stop wayward thoughts from arising, and you instructed me: 'Let them just arise or cease as they will.' But, since then, although I've taken your advice to heart, I've found it hard to let my thoughts just arise or cease like this."

The Master told him: "The reason you're having difficulty is that you think there's some special *way* to let your thoughts just arise or cease as they will."

(*zenshū*, p. 129.)

Just as you are

The Master addressed the assembly: "All of you should realize the vital, functioning, living Buddha Mind! For several hundred years now, [people in] both China and Japan have misunderstood the Zen teaching, trying to attain enlightenment by doing zazen or trying to find 'the one who sees and hears,' all of which is a great mistake. Zazen is just another name for original mind, and means to sit in tranquility with a tranquil mind. When you do sitting meditation, you're simply sitting, just as you are; when you do walking meditation, you're walking, just as you are. Even if your mouth were big enough to swallow heaven and earth, Buddhism couldn't be expressed in words. Those who do speak about Buddhism, for the most part, are only blinding people's eyes.

"In the mind you have from your parents innately, there isn't even a trace of delusion. So when you fail to realize this and insist, 'I'm deluded because I'm an unenlightened being,' you're unjustly accusing your own parents as well! The buddhas of the past and the people of today are one. There's no difference between them. Let me give you an example: When water from the ocean is ladled into different sorts of tubs and the weather turns cold, the water freezes, and, according to whether the tub is large or small, round or square, the ice will assume different shapes; yet when the ice melts, all the water is the same as the [water of the] ocean. Not knowing the living and functioning buddha, you think you'll *become* a buddha by accumulating the fruits of religious practice and realizing 'enlightenment,' lost in error, going from darkness into darkness. Pathetic, isn't it? I don't teach about Buddhism, but when I talk to you just deal with all your wrong ideas."

(*zenshū*, p. 130.)

Not even a trace

A visiting monk asked: "I'm performing religious practice with the aim of realizing enlightenment. What do you think about this?"

The Master said: "Enlightenment only exists in contrast to delusion. And since everyone possesses the substance of buddhahood, not even a trace of delusion exists. So what is it you need to realize?"

The monk said: "That seems foolish to me. It was by realizing enlightenment that all the ancient sages, beginning with Daruma himself, experienced complete attainment of the Dharma."

The Master told him: "It's by being 'foolish' that the tathagata saves sentient beings. To neither come nor go, but to remain just as you innately are, without allowing the mind to become obscured—this is what's meant by tathagata. And such was the way with all the patriarchs of the past."

(zenshū, p. 130.)

*   *   *

Kantarō's question

At one time the Master was staying at the Kannon temple at Kiyodani in Iyo's Kita district.[4] The headman of the nearby village of Utsu,[5] one Kantarō, came regularly to study with him. Although Kantarō occasionally tried to stump the Master with difficult questions, the Master's sharp and piercing response remained far beyond his reach.

One day, Kantarō set out to visit Kiyodani in the company of Yoshino Yojizaemon.[6] On their way, he said to Yoshino: "Whenever I go to see him, the Master says: 'Kantarō, have you come?' I'm sure today will be the same as always. So, if the Master says, 'Kantarō, have you come?' I'll say, 'Who could *that* fellow be?' "

The two arrived at Kiyodani. The Master came and greeted Yoshino, but said nothing to Kantarō. After some time, Kantarō said: "Well, is your Reverence feeling all right?"

The Master replied: "Who could *that* fellow be?"
Kantarō, wholly at a loss, expressed his apologies.

(*zenshū*, p. 131.)

Jōsen

The monk Jōsen[7] said: "I'm greatly troubled by [the problem of] death, and that's why I come regularly to see your Reverence. I think that, for a human being, there is no matter of greater importance."

The Master said: "This spirit is the basis for the study of Buddhism. If you hold to it and don't lose your determination, you'll be directly in accord with the Way."

[Jōsen] asked: "What does it mean to realize buddhahood?"

The Master replied: "Fully affirm what I've told you, have faith in it and harbor no doubts, and then you'll be realizing buddhahood."

Some time later, [Jōsen] remarked: "Lately, I felt that my mind was vast and boundless as the sky, without being fixed anywhere. 'This must be it!' I thought, but, on reflection, I realized that I had better not tarry there."

The Master said: "That is your discrimination. Realize what is *before* discrimination."

On yet another occasion, Jōsen said: "I feel fortunate that my determination has been particularly strong of late."

The Master replied: "Such things too are bound to happen."

Once the Zen teacher Tairyō[8] said [to Jōsen]: "You seem to be earnest, but you're always [repeating] the same thing."[9]

Jōsen said: "Not at all. It's simply something I never tire of hearing."

Just then, the Master came out and took his seat. "Whenever you have the chance to hear this," he said, "it's worth hearing, no matter how many times; so don't think it's [just a repetition of] the same thing. When you feel something is valuable, then every time you *hear* it it's valuable."

(*zenshū*, pp. 131–132.)

The gambler

In Aboshi there was a man named Hachirōbei. He said [to the Master]: "As a member of the True Pure Land Sect, I rely wholeheartedly on the Tathagata Amida, and knowing his saving grace to be certain, I recite the *nembutsu* of gratitude."

The Master replied: "If, praying for Amida's saving grace, you constantly go around gambling and doing all sorts of evil things, that's like cheating Amida."

At the time, this Hachirōbei was a notorious gambler. Those present were all impressed.

(*zenshū*, p. 132.)

Miracles

On another occasion, Hachirōbei came and said: "The teachers of old performed all sorts of miracles. Can your Reverence perform miracles too?"

The Master replied: "What sort of things were these 'miracles?' "

Hachirōbei said: "In Echigo, the founder of the True Pure Land Sect[10] had someone hold up a piece of paper on one side of the river, and when he took up his brush on the opposite bank, he perfectly inscribed the six characters *namu amida butsu,* so that to this day everyone speaks reverently of the *'nembutsu* that crossed the river.' "

The Master laughed and said: "If that's the sort of thing you mean, people who practice magic and the like can do even better! Really, to bring up the doings of such people in a place for the true teaching of Buddhism is [like] trying to compare dogs and cats to men."

(zenshū, p. 132.)

A visiting monk

Several visiting monks came, and at their interview with the Master each presented his understanding. Among them was one fellow who remained silent. The Master said: "Well, how about *you?*"

The monk said: "As for me, when cold, I put on more clothes; when hungry, I take something to eat; when thirsty, I drink some hot water; other than that—nothing."

The Master said: "Well, in that case, can you tell the degree of understanding of the people who are here now?"

The monk replied: "Certainly I can."

The Master said: "How does it look to you, then, the understanding of the people around you here?"

The monk said: "You show me *my* understanding."

The Master replied: "Everything we've been discussing [*shows*] your understanding."

The monk prostrated himself three times and went off.

(zenshū, p. 132.)

Being/non-being

A visiting monk came forward and declared: "It's not in being, it's not in non-being, it's not in absolute emptiness."

The Master said: "Right at this moment, where *is* it?"

Completely flustered, the monk withdrew.

(*zenshū*, p. 133.)

Why are we born?

A layman asked: "If we're endowed with the Buddha Mind, why is it we don't *remain* buddhas, but are born and experience all sorts of suffering?"

The Master said: "That you came to be born is your *parents'* mistake."

(*zenshū*, p. 133.)

The one who sees and hears

A layman asked: "For years now I've entrusted myself to the teaching of the old masters, [trying to answer the question] 'Who is the one who sees and hears?'[11] What sort of practice can I do to find 'the one who sees and hears'? I've searched and searched, but today I still haven't found him."

The Master said: "Since my school is the School of Buddha Mind, there's no duality between 'the one who sees and hears' and the one who searches [for him]. If you search outside, you'll never find him, even if you travel the whole world through. The One Mind, unborn—this is 'the one' that, in everybody, sees images in the eyes, hears sounds in the ears and, generally, when it encounters the objects of the six senses, reveals whatever is seen or heard, felt or thought, with nothing left concealed."

(*zenshū*, p. 133.)

The woman afraid of thunder

A woman asked: "I'm uncommonly frightened of thunder, and the moment I hear it, I feel awful and suffer miserably.[12] Please teach me how I can stop being afraid like this."

The Master said: "When you were born, there was no sense of being afraid of things, there was only the Unborn Buddha Mind. Deluded notions of being afraid of things are phantoms of thought created *after* you were born. Thunder causes rain to fall on the world for the benefit of mankind; it's not something that's hostile to people. Your regarding that thunder as something to be afraid of is the doing of those phantoms of thought, it's not due to anything outside. When you hear the thunder, you should have absolute faith in your own mind's buddhahood."

(*zenshū*, p. 133.)

Bereavement

A woman questioned the Master: "I am miserable over the death of my child. If I even see a child the same age, it reminds me of him, and then all sorts of things fill my mind and my deluded thoughts go on and on. Please teach me."

The Master said: "When you recall things like this, it's something you are *doing*. In the original mind, there's not even a trace of different delusions. Have faith in what I'm saying, and you'll become a person who's originally free."

(*zenshū*, pp. 133–134.)

Blinding your eyes

A visiting monk asked: "Is there any merit in practicing zazen?"

The Master said: "Zazen isn't to be despised, nor are reciting sutras, performing prostrations and so on. Tokusan used the stick, Rinzai uttered the *katsu!*, Gutei raised his finger and Daruma faced the wall—but, while different, all these were just the masters' expedients, methods to confront particular situations and deal with the individual needs [of the students involved]. Right from the start, there have never been fixed rules. If you take these [temporary expedients] as invariable teachings, you'll be blinding your own eyes. Simply have firm faith in what I say, remaining as you innately are without making idle distinctions, just like when things are reflected in a mirror, and then there's nothing in the world you won't penetrate through and through. Do not doubt!"

(*zenshū*, p. 134.)

Everything is smoothly managed

A Zen monk from Tamba asked: "It's my sincere desire on this occasion to realize buddhahood and become a perfect person in all respects. Please let me have your instruction."

The Master said: "You've come a long distance, but while these aspirations of yours are commendable, they're all delusion. In original mind, there are no delusions, no aspirations. In the intrinsic, marvelously illuminating dynamic function, there aren't any aspirations at all, and yet everything is smoothly managed. Even wanting to attain buddhahood right away is something artificial. When you realize that you're producing all aspirations yourself and, without getting involved with particular things, remain just as you innately are, your own intrinsic nature will be revealed."

(*zenshū*, p. 134.)

Where do you go?

A layman asked: "If you become a buddha, where do you go?"

The Master replied: "If you become a buddha, there's no place at all to go. You fill the vast universe[13] to its very limits. It's when you become any other sort of being that there are different places to go."

(zenshū, p. 134.)

The golden ball

Once the Master said: "Unlike the other masters everywhere, in my teaching I don't set up any particular object, such as realizing enlightenment or studying koans. Nor do I rely on the words of the buddhas and patriarchs. I just point things out directly, so there's nothing to hold onto, and that's why no one will readily accept [what I teach]. To begin with, those who are wise and learned are obstructed by their own cleverness and calculation, so for them it's impossible to accept. On the other hand, there are lots of ignorant women who can neither read nor write, who haven't any special ability and can't be pushed on to become Zen masters, but possess a truly heartfelt realization and don't engage in intellectualizing."

He added: "Even if there's no one who accepts it completely, my teaching is like a golden ball that's been smashed to pieces and scattered about, so that anyone who gets one piece has one piece of illumination, anyone who gets two pieces, two pieces of illumination, and so on, bit by bit, with no one who won't benefit according to his own portion [of attainment].

(zenshū, pp. 134–135.)

Thinking

A layman asked: "I've heard that your Reverence is able to see into people's minds. Right at this moment, what am I thinking?"

The Master said: "You're thinking precisely *that*."
(*zenshū*, p. 135.)

* * *

Women

A woman asked: "I've heard that because women bear a heavy karmic burden it's impossible for them to realize buddhahood. Is this true?"
The Master said: "From what time did you become a 'woman?' "

A woman said: "Because women bear a heavy karmic burden, they are forbidden from entering esteemed temples like Mount Koya[14] and Mount Hiei."[15]
The Master told her: "In Kamakura there's a temple for nuns,[16] and there *men* are forbidden."
(*zenshū*, p. 135.)

The merchant's dream

When the Master was staying at the Ryōmonji, a lay acquaintance of Zenkō[17] from Ōmi[18] came to the temple and remained for some time. At his first interview with the Master, he accepted the essentials of his teaching, and thereafter simply followed along with the others, listening to the Master's sermons.

Once, when the Master was receiving a group of new arrivals in the abbot's quarters, this layman came forward and said: "My home is such-and-such a village in the province of Ōmi. Originally I was a *rōnin*, and, taking what savings I had in gold and silver, I lent out money and grain to the people of the area and with the interest on these loans made my living. However, a little over ten years ago, I left my business to my son, and, building a retreat in my garden, devoted myself to performing zazen and reciting sutras. I also went to study with various Zen masters, practicing single-mindedly. Zenkō is well-acquainted with these things.

"However, last night, in a dream, I found myself back at home, reading sutras at the household shrine. Just then, a customer who had borrowed some rice came to pay his interest, and together with my son set about calculating the amount. In the midst of reading the sutras, I realized there was an error in their calculations, and just as I was telling them of it, I suddenly awoke from my dream. Thinking over this, [I realize] just how deep and difficult to destroy are the roots of karmic nature. What sort of practice can I do to destroy my basic sinfulness?"

The layman was moved to tears by the strength of his feelings. Everyone present was impressed.

The Master said: "Was this a good dream or a bad dream?"

The layman replied: "A bad dream. It was for this that more than twenty years ago I abandoned all mercenary affairs to dwell in oneness with buddhadharma, in circumstances of purity and tranquility, far from the tumult of worldly life. *This* is the sort of thing I [would expect to] see in my dreams; yet I'm afraid the fact that what came to me were my old concerns of twenty years ago shows these things have permeated my innermost mind,[19] and that distresses me."

The Master said: "This is what's known as being had by a dream."

The layman rose and prostrated himself. "Today for the first time," he declared, "I have been freed from endless kalpas of birth and death!" And, reeling with joy, he went off.

(*zenshū*, p. 136.)

It's fine just to feel that way

A layman said: "I sometimes feel startled when I'm surprised by some sound, such as a clap of thunder. Is this because I'm not in control all the time? How can I guard against this so that, no matter what happens, I won't feel startled?"

The Master said: "If you feel startled, it's fine just to feel that way. When you try to guard against it, you're creating duality."

(zenshū, p. 136.)

Using the three inches

A monk asked: "Tokusan has his stick, Rinzai, his shout[20]—all the old masters employed the stick and the shout, but your Reverence doesn't use them at all. How do you explain this?"

The Master said: "Tokusan and Rinzai knew how to use the stick and the shout; I know how to use the three inches [of my tongue]."

(zenshū, p. 136.)

Koans

A monk asked: "[Former masters] such as Engo and Daie[21] used koans in teaching their students. How is it your Reverence makes no use of them?"

The Master said: "How about the Zen teachers *before* Daie and Engo, did *they* use koans?"[22]

(zenshū, p. 137.)

The great doubt

A monk asked: "The men of old declared that with a great doubt one will experience a great enlightenment. How is it your Reverence doesn't make use of the great doubt of the masters?"

The Master replied: "As to what's meant by 'great doubt': long ago when Nangaku[23] went to see the Sixth Patriarch, he was asked by him, 'What is it that comes thus?' Nangaku was utterly flustered, but puzzling over this for eight years, [finally] answered: 'As soon as you speak about a thing, you miss the mark.' This is the real great doubt and great enlightenment. For example, when a monk loses his only *kesa*[24] and, searching and searching, can't put it out of his mind for even a moment—that's real doubt! People nowadays go stirring up doubt just because they say the old masters did, so what they produce is an imitation doubt. Because this doubt isn't genuine, they won't have any day of awakening. It's just as if they were to search all over, thinking they'd lost something that had never been lost at all."

(*zenshū*, p. 137.)

Is this buddha?

[When the Master] was at the Gyokuryūji[25] in Mino, a layman came forward, gave a shout and demanded: "Is this buddha?"

The Master took his fan and pressing it against the fellow's head, [said]: "Do you know what this is?"

The layman replied: "This is buddha."

Once more taking up his fan, the Master poked it into the layman's cheek, saying: "You only know the *name* buddha."

Utterly taken aback, the fellow withdrew.

(*zenshū*, p. 137.)

*　　*　　*

Layman Chōzen

Chōzen,[26] father of the monk Jiton of the Osaka Kanzanji[27] and [formerly] headman of the village of Taima in Washū,[28] lived in retirement and was known as a longtime student of Zen. For many years he had been a follower of the Ōbaku Zen Master Ryūkei[29] and was famous as a lay Buddhist. He would also come frequently to visit the Master at the Kanzanji, but they knew each other so well that [the Master] had never engaged him in dialogue to actually test his understanding. Once when the Master was at the Jizōji in Kyoto, Chōzen came to see him, and in the course of his visit, the Master said: "Well, Chōzen, how is your practice?"

Chōzen replied: "I've been completing my practice in a rather extraordinary way: I regularly eat fish and meat, I drink wine, I gamble at *go*; I go to sleep, I get up—my world is free and easy and without constraint."

The Master said: "You probably won't listen, but let me tell you *my* style [of Zen]." And, so saying, he instructed [Chōzen]. Chōzen withdrew in silence and stayed the night, sharing the quarters of the monk Soboku,[30] who reported that he seemed agitated the whole evening and had not slept at all.

At that time, it was the turn of the Zen Master Bokuō[31] to assume the abbacy of the headquarters temple,[32] and the Master set off before daybreak to pay his respects. A servant came back with word that the Master would return at sundown. Just as Soboku and Chōzen came out together to the entryway to meet him, the Master passed by, [going] directly into the abbot's quarters and proceeding to the inner room, where he seated himself. Chōzen immediately went before the Master and prostrated himself three times.

The Master joined his palms and said: "I accept the bow [that acknowledges] the constant observance of religious abstention.[33] This is the way it must be for one who takes refuge in the buddhadharma."

Once again Chōzen prostrated himself three times.

The Master said: "I receive the bow [that acknowledges] abstention from wine. This too is the way it must be, since it is the rule established by the Buddha."

Chōzen said: "Master Reigan always praised you as a clear-eyed teacher, but I couldn't believe it. The men of old were like this, but I never dreamed that among the teachers of today there could be anyone whose eyes were clear. 'Disgusting!' I thought skeptically. Now I've seen how wrong I was, having met with this undreamed-of opportunity." And, shedding tears, he became the Master's disciple.

Some time after this, when the Master was once again stopping at the Kanzanji, Jiton and Chōzen came to see him, and Jiton humbly expressed his gratitude, saying: "Because of your Reverence's kind instruction, Chōzen has become a man of perfect freedom in all his daily activities."[34]

The Master said: "People all value enlightenment, but Chōzen was lucky enough to *destroy* enlightenment and become a man of perfect freedom."

(*zenshū*, pp. 139–140.)

The craftsman's dilemma

A layman asked: "I'm a founder by trade. When I make pots and kettles, eight out of ten have holes, but I patch them up and sell them, saying they're perfect. This weighs on my mind. Is it a crime?"

The Master said: "Are you the only one who does this sort of thing?"

"Not at all," he replied, "everyone else does exactly the same."

The Master asked: "Do you sell your wares at night?"

The founder answered: "I sell in broad daylight."

The Master said: "The people who bought your things did so with their eyes open. If you were to sell your wares at night, claiming damaged pieces to be perfect, that would be criminal, but since it's happening in broad daylight, these people shouldn't buy such things if they know they're damaged. You needn't accuse yourself unnecessarily over this business."

(zenshū, p. 140.)

*   *   *

The angry abbot

One winter, during the training period at the Sanyūji in Bizen,[35] laymen and monks from both Bizen and Bitchū[36] assembled in large numbers on the days when the Master would appear to lecture. At Niwase[37] in Bitchū was a large temple of the Lotus sect,[38] whose eminent abbot was a scholar of great learning much revered by the parishioners. At that time, the Master's teaching was sweeping the area, and the abbot's parishioners all went to hear him. The abbot, seething with indignation, told his congregation: "From what I hear, this Bankei is an uneducated fellow. If I go and put a difficult question to him, I can stymie him with just one word."

So saying, he went off one day to see the Master. He stood at the back of the assembly and in the middle of the

Master's talk shouted in a booming voice: "Everyone here accepts your sermon and believes it. [But] someone like myself doesn't accept the essentials of your teaching. If a person doesn't accept them, how are you going to save him?"

The Master raised his fan and said: "Come forward."

The abbot stepped before him.

The Master said: "Now come a little closer."

The abbot moved forward again.

The Master said: "How well you accept what I say!"

The abbot, completely flustered, left without another word.

(zenshū, p. 142.)

*   *   *

When I first began to search

Once the Master said: "When I first began to search for enlightenment, I wasn't able to find a good teacher and, as a result, did all sorts of painful practices, pouring out my heart's blood. Sometimes I'd forsake the company of men and go into seclusion; at other times I'd fashion a paper mosquito net and, sitting inside it, practice meditation; or else I'd shutter all the windows and meditate in my darkened room. Without permitting myself to lie down, I'd sit cross-legged until my thighs became inflamed with sores, the marks of which remained with me even afterward. At the same time, if I happened to hear a good teacher was to be found in some place or other, I'd set off at once to meet him. In this way I spent several years, and I think I may say there were few places in Japan that I didn't leave my footprints. And all because I wasn't able to meet an accomplished teacher! Once I'd hit on enlightenment, I realized for the first time that I'd been struggling uselessly all those years, and was able to achieve tranquility. I tell you all that, without any struggle, you can attain complete realization now right where you are, but you won't believe me because you're not truly serious about the Dharma."

(*zenshū*, p. 143.)

All the difference of heaven and earth

On another occasion, the Master said: "When it comes to the truth I uncovered when I was twenty-six[39] and living in retreat at the village of Nonaka[40] in Akō in Harima— the truth for which I went to see Dōsha and obtained his confirmation—so far as the truth is concerned, between that time and this, from beginning to end, there hasn't been a shred of difference. However, so far as penetrating the great truth of Buddhism with the perfect clarity of the Dharma Eye[41] and realizing absolute freedom, between the time I met Dōsha and today, there's all the difference of heaven and earth! All of you must have faith that this sort of thing can happen, and live in expectation of the day when you'll completely realize the Dharma Eye."

[Someone] asked: "Will the perfect clarity of the Dharma Eye be realized completely with time? Does one just attain it all at once?"

The Master replied: "There's no question of there being a particular [amount of] time. When the Eye of the Way is clear, without a single flaw, you'll have realized it completely. And your realizing it will be due to your earnest and single-minded cultivation."

(*zenshū*, pp. 143–144.)

Watch where you're going

When I[42] first met the Master, I received his teaching, but failing to gain a penetrating understanding, I said:

"What your Reverence teaches is from the realm of the master. But for a fellow like me who's never experienced great enlightenment, I'm afraid that reaching the master's realm is going to be hard."

The Master told me: "If you want the Truth, you should do as I say. Students of the Way must first of all take care to watch where they're going. For example, if someone is going to Edo and learns he should travel east, after going one mile, he's one mile closer, and so on for five and then ten miles, until finally he's sure to arrive there. [But] if he mistakenly sets off to the west, even if it's just a single step [at first], the more he exerts himself, the further from Edo he'll be."

(*zenshū*, p. 144.)

The proof

Once I asked the Master: "Is it helpful in studying the Way to read through the Buddhist sutras and the records of the old masters?"

The Master said: "It all depends. If you rely on the principles contained in the sutras and records, when you read them, you'll be blinding your own eyes. On the other hand, when the time comes that you can *dismiss* principles, if you read [such things], you'll find the proof of your own realization."

(*zenshū*, p. 144.)

*　　*　　*

True acceptance

Once I asked the Master: "I've always been plagued by bad habits. Can I stop my bad habits by guarding against them at all times?"

The Master said: "If you realize that originally there *are* no bad habits, what is there to stop?"

I replied: "I accept that originally there are no bad habits and haven't any doubts on that score. All the same, my bad habits manifest themselves from time to time, and when I guard against them, this doesn't happen. So, even if I thoroughly accept the fact that originally bad habits don't exist, when it comes to my daily life practice, isn't it still best to guard against them?"

The Master said: "This is not true acceptance."

Now, ever since I have taken to heart the Master's kind words, I have conclusively realized the actual manifestation of the truth.

(*zenshū*, p. 145.)

My old illness

On another occasion, I asked: "Since birth I've suffered from terrible spasms of pain in my stomach. When they occur, I have to stop eating entirely for several days, experience dreadful headaches and feel so miserable I can't even put my hand out to straighten the pillow. Ordinarily when I'm feeling fine I forge dauntlessly ahead, ready to sacrifice life and limb for the sake of the Dharma, but, at times like this, just a touch of my old illness renders me helpless. When the pain is at its height, I'm weaker than ever. It's as if my usual vigorous spirit were at the mercy of the wind. When I come up against my old illness, I feel completely devastated. I'm terribly distressed about this."

The Master said: "How is it once your health returns?"

I replied: "When I'm well again, everything is back to normal."

The Master said: "Then that's fine."

Thereafter, at all times, I've remained just as I am,

beyond discrimination, free and easy and without constraint.

(zenshū, pp. 145–146.)

Seven out of ten

Once I questioned the Master: "For some time I have followed your Reverence, and for several years have been fortunate enough to serve at your side as attendant. When it comes to the essentials of your teaching, I have no doubts at all. However, what I find remarkable in observing your Reverence at close hand is that 'The deeper I penetrate, the more solid you become; the more I look up, the higher you soar,' so that I ceaselessly 'sigh in admiration.'[43] Your freedom in responding to the needs of students is so limitless that it seems as if one could never match it however many days and months passed. How can we [too] achieve perfection?"

The Master said: "Zen students as a rule may grasp seven or eight things in ten, but are unable to get past [the remaining] two or three."

I said: "What is the way to get past?"

The Master replied: "There is no way to get past."

I asked: "Seeing as there's no way to get past and one is unable to do so, where can the fault be?"

The Master remained silent for a time, and then replied: "When you come right down to it, it's because the desire [to realize] the great truth of Buddhism is weak."

(zenshū, p. 146.)

*   *   *

The monk Zeshin

The monk Zeshin[44] lived in religious retreat on Mt. Yoshino[45] for many years, devoting himself solely to meditation [till] one day he suddenly awoke and forgot everything he knew. At a neighboring temple lived a venerable monk of the Sōtō school, and [Zeshin] went and presented his understanding, seeking the monk's confirmation of his attainment.

The monk said: "At the present time, the Zen Master Bankei is a clear-eyed teacher. Go study with him."

[Zeshin] then went immediately to the Kyoto Jizōji in Higashiyama. At that time, the Master was practicing in retreat, so that there was no one to receive [Zeshin] and present his request. Nevertheless, every day he would come and sit in meditation outside the temple gate, returning to Kyoto in the evening. When he had continued like this for thirteen days, the landlord at the inn questioned him about it. Zeshin told him everything, and the innkeeper directed him to visit the Zen Teacher Dokushō[46] in Saga. Zeshin then went to meet Dokushō and presented his understanding.

Dokushō said: "Preserve it with care!"

That very day, [Zeshin] left [Kyoto] and returned to Yoshino. Several months had passed when he decided to set off [again] for the Jizōji. On his way, he learned that, just then, the Master was in Edo, so he went straightaway to the Kōrinji. The Master received him immediately, and Zeshin presented his understanding.

The Master demanded: "The Ultimate!"

Zeshin, at a loss, made a low bow. When this had been repeated three times, Zeshin said: "*Is* there an Ultimate?"

The Master replied: "You don't know how to use it."

Zeshin, once again at a loss, bowed deeply. After this had been repeated three times, Zeshin asked: "What *is* the way to use it?"

Just at that moment, an *uguisu*[47] sang in the garden. The Master said: "When the *uguisu* sings, you hear it."

Zeshin, overcome with joy, prostrated himself three times.

The Master told him: "From here on, never open your mouth needlessly."

At the end of the summer training period, the Master returned to the Ryōmonji, and Zeshin followed him to the temple. Several days later, at a reception for newly arrived monks, Zeshin came forward and presented himself before the Master, but [the Master] ignored him. For three days [the Master] came out like this and for three days too Zeshin continued to present himself, but without a word from the Master.

[One day,] when everyone had gone, the Master turned to Zeshin and said: "You're a lucky fellow. If you hadn't met me, you'd have surely become a boastful goblin!"

Zeshin then begged to be admitted to the temple, and, at his request, received the name Ryōko. Afterwards, at the urging of the assembly, he took the name Daien.

(zenshū, pp. 147–148.)

FROM THE GYŌGŌ
RYAKKI

Suspicion

During the [Great Training Period at the Ryōmonji], there was an incident in which some money was lost in the Fudō Hall.[1] One day, when the Master ascended the lecture seat, a monk came forward and said: "I am such-and-such a person of . . . province and a student at the . . . temple. This winter I have been practicing in the Fudō Hall. A monk in the place next to mine lost his traveling money, and because I was in the seat beside his, suspected me of taking it. The rumor has spread through the entire hall, and I beg your Reverence to conduct an inquiry."

The Master asked: "Did you steal anything?"

The monk replied: "At a unique religious gathering like this, such a shameless act would never even cross my mind!"

The Master told him: "Then everything is all right."

The monk said: "Yes, but at this meeting, monks are gathered from all over Japan, and I'm worried that if there is no inquiry, I'll be given a bad name throughout the country. I beseech your Reverence's kind understanding."

The Master said: "If there's an inquiry, the guilty one will have to come out—is that all right too?"

The monk then declared: "It's *I* who have shown the very worst kind of shamefulness, being self-centered and arrogant in a case like this after I'd listened to your won-

derful teaching every day!" And, shedding tears of gratitude, he withdrew.

(zenshū, pp. 396–397.)

Handling delinquents

When the Master was in retreat at the Jizōji, Sekimon
Oshō[2] of the Ryōmonji sent [the monk] Tenkyū[3] to call on
him and inquire after his health.[4] When he met the Master at the temple gate, Tenkyū delivered a message from
Sekimon, saying: "At the Ryōmonji are a number of nov-
ices who are remiss in their duties and rude in their behavior, upsetting the decorum of the temple. It was thought
that if they were to go someplace else—the Nyohōji, perhaps, or the Kōrinji—they might change their ways, and I
wished to ask your Reverence's opinion."

When Tenkyū had spoken, the Master summoned
Shūin, Sōkaku and myself,[5] and, repeating for us the gist
of the message Sekimon had sent with Tenkyū, said: "What's
known as a Zen temple is established precisely to bring
together wicked fellows such as these, winning them over
through personal contact and making them into good men.
But, without any such attitude, completely lacking in
compassion, you want to dispose of wrongdoers elsewhere,
to have them go and create disturbance someplace else! Is
a person like that fit to be abbot of a Zen temple? When
one whose heart is without generosity or compassion becomes abbot of [my] temple, it is the beginning of the end
for my teaching!"

After this severe upbraiding, everyone, whether it was
the abbot, the temple officers or the Master's personal attendants, was afraid to complain to the Master about the
behavior of the monks.

(zenshū, p. 396.)

The missing paper

When the Master was in Shinyashiki[6] in Aboshi, he was unable to find a memorandum he needed. His attendants searched about everywhere, but they too failed to turn it up. Later, they discovered it at last. At that time, the Master scolded them, saying: "If you had all, right from the beginning, determined to find it, even if you tore the house down, it would have quickly turned up. But since you went about it half-heartedly, you were unable to locate it. While this memo is nothing of great importance, my having you search for it was to cultivate in you the sort of resolute attitude that you will carry with you through life. With a half-hearted frame of mind, you won't become even half a man!"

Afterwards, when the Master was staying at the Ōshiken,[7] he was [preparing to] inscribe a Buddhist name[8] and found the brush to be missing. Although his attendants searched about in every possible way, they failed to turn it up, and this time, once again, he scolded them as he had before.

(*zenshū*, p. 398.)

POEMS

Chinese poems

Instructing the Assembly

Chasing after words, pursuing phrases, when will you
ever be done?
You run yourself ragged amassing knowledge,
becoming widely informed
Self-nature is empty and illuminating, so let things
take care of themselves
There's nothing else I have to pass on
(*zenshū*, p. 496.)

Impromptu Poem

Not angry when abused, not happy when praised
A great blockhead of the universe!
Going along as circumstances carry me—north, south,
east, west
Without hiding my ugliness and clumsiness between
heaven and earth
(*zenshū*, p. 499.)

Instructing a Confucian of Bizen

It ranges over past and present, pervades the entire
universe
Look and it's not to be seen, [but] call and it responds
A stringless lute, a silent melody
This has nothing to do with being a monk or a layman
(*zenshū*, p. 497.)

New Years
  What does it matter, the new year, the old year?
  I stretch out my legs and all alone have a quiet sleep
  Don't tell me the monks aren't getting their instruction
  Here and there the nightingale is singing: the highest
              Zen![1]
                      (*zenshū*, p. 498.)

Instructions to a Confucian
  From the outset, the Great Way knows no distinction
              between worldly and
              transcendental
  Let Buddhism and Confucianism return to the source,
              and all differences cease to exist
  When you penetrate directly, beyond words and letters
  Going forward or backward, whatever you do creates a
              refreshing breeze[2]
                      (*zenshū*, p. 497.)

Instructing the Assembly
  Mind accords with all circumstances, yet doesn't arise
              or cease
  The sages of old praised this, calling it *zazen*
  Blind people wear out their cushions waiting for
              enlightenment
  Just like trying to make a mirror by polishing a brick
                      (*zenshū*, p. 495.)

Instructions to the Layman Gessō[3] in Response to his
              Questions on the Technique of
              the Lance
  The Great Function manifests itself without fixed rules
  Meeting each situation on its own terms, it's never too
              soon, never too late
  Thrusting, retracting, advancing, retreating—it all
              takes place beyond the realm of
              thought

When you're in harmony with Mind, arms and legs
operate on their own

(*zenshū*, p. 496.)

Japanese Poems

The Preaching of Insentient Things
  In spring, the cherry blossoms
  In fall, the autumn leaves
  The various forms of nature, just as they are
  All of them, the words of the Law

(*zenshū*, p. 515.)

Impromptu Poem
  Good is awful
  Bad is awful
  And awful is awful too
  Things and events
  Are only the product of circumstances

(*zenshū*, p. 516.)

My Meditation Hut
  (*This poem was probably composed while Bankei was
still in his early teens, during the period after his expulsion
from home by his elder brother in exasperation at Bankei's
repeated truancy from the local school. Eventually Bankei's
plight attracted the sympathy of an old family friend, Nakabori Sukeyasu, headman of the neighboring village of Shimomura.*[4] *Sukeyasu had befriended Bankei's father when
he first arrived in the area as a masterless samurai, and he
now erected a hermitage for Bankei on the mountain over-
looking the Nakabori family home, where the young seeker
became a frequent guest [see "Words and Deeds," pp. 145–
46]. Besides providing Bankei with a hospitable refuge while*

he struggled to resolve the questions that had driven him from the village school and into Buddhism, the hut evidently commanded a spectacular view of the Inland Sea and the Ejima Archipelago, which here directly faces the coastline.)

As I glance about
The haze settles:
Here revealed through dense mists
Here through thin
Spring daybreak over the Ejima Islands
(*zenshū*, p. 515.)

Song of Original Mind (Honshin no uta)
(Bankei is said to have composed this series of verses in 1653 when he was living in retreat in the mountains of Yoshino. Different versions and arrangements of the verses exist, and it is not known which represents the poem's original form. One text states that Bankei composed the poem as instruction for the local children. Another gives the explanation that to combat a severe drought which afflicted the area, Bankei had the villagers, young and old alike, sing the verses as they danced at the local shrine. The result was a plentiful rainfall, and thereafter the performance of Bankei's "rain song" became a local tradition. This account explains why the poem is also known as Amagoi-uta, "Praying-for-Rain Song," *and* Odori-uta, "Dance Song." *It is, however, unclear why it sometimes appears under the title* Usuhiki-uta, *or "Milling Song," a type of song sung while grinding flour.)*

Unborn and imperishable
Is the original mind
Earth, water, fire and wind[5]
A temporary lodging for the night

Attached to this
    Ephemeral burning house[6]
You yourselves light the fire, kindle the
                    flames
    In which you're consumed

Search back
    To the time
When you were born
    You can't remember a thing at all!

Keep your mind as it was
    When you came into the world
And instantly this very self[7]
    Is a living "thus-come" one[8]

Ideas of
What's good, what's bad
All due to
This self of yours

In winter, a bonfire
    Spells delight
But when summertime arrives
    What a nuisance it becomes!

And the breezes
    You loved in summer
Even before autumn's gone
    Already have become a bother

When you've got money
    You despise the poor
But have you forgotten how it was
    Back when you were poor yourself?

The money you amassed in life
    Amassed with a demonic heart
You'll watch with horror and alarm
    Seized upon by hungry ghosts

Throwing your whole life away
    Sacrificed to the thirst for gold
But when you saw your life was through
    All your money was no use

Clinging, craving and the like
    I don't have them on my mind
That's why nowadays I can say
    The whole world is truly mine!

Your longing for the one you love
    Is for the present time alone
It only exists by reason of
    The past before she'd come along

To recall someone
    Means you can't forget
Not to recall them
    That you never had forgot

Thinking back over the past
    You find it was an evening's dream
Realize that, and you'll see
    Everything is just a lie

Those who feel embittered by
    Life in this floating world of grief
Anguish themselves, distress their minds
    Brooding over empty dreams

Since, after all, this floating world
    Is unreal

Instead of holding onto things in
    Your mind, go and sing!

Only original mind exists
    In the past and in the future too
Instead of holding onto things in
    Your mind, let them go!

When you don't attach to things
    The floating world will cease to be
Nothing is left, nothing at all
    That's what "living tathagata" means

Having created
    The demon mind yourself
When it torments you mercilessly
    You're to blame and no one else

When you do wrong
    Your mind's the demon
There's no hell
    To be found outside

Abominating hell
    Longing for heaven
You make yourself suffer
    In a joyful world

You think that good
    Means hating what is bad
What's bad is
    The hating mind itself

Good, you say,
    Means doing good
Bad indeed
    The mind that says so!

Good and bad alike
        Roll them both into one ball
Wrap it up in paper and then
        Toss it out—forget it all!

Mysteries and miracles—
        There are no such things!
But when you fail to understand
        The world's full of weird happenings

This is the phantom
        Who deceives
Who makes us take the false world
        To be real

Fame, wealth, eating and drinking, sleep
                        and sensual
                                delight—
        Once you've learned the Five
                        Desires
They become
        Your guide in life

Notions of what one should do
        Never existed from the start
Fighting about what's right, what's wrong
        That's the doing of the *I*

When your study
        Of Buddhism is through
You find
        You haven't anything new

Enlightenment and delusion too
        Never existed at the start

They're ideas that you picked up
　　　Things your parents never taught[9]

If you think the mind
　　　That attains enlightenment
Is "mine"
　　　Your thoughts will wrestle, one with
　　　　　　　　the other

These days I'm not bothering about
　　　Getting enlightenment all the time
And the result is that
　　　I wake up in the morning feeling
　　　　　　　　fine!

Praying for salvation in the world to come
　　　Praying for your own selfish ends
Is only piling on more and more
　　　Self-centeredness and arrogance

Nowadays I'm tired of
　　　Praying for salvation too
I just move along at my ease
　　　Letting the breath come and go

Die—then live
　　　Day and night within the world
Once you've done this, then you can
　　　Hold the world right in your hand!

It's the buddhas I feel sorry for:
　　　With all those ornaments they wear
They must be
　　　Dazzled by the glare!

Still too soon for you to be
　　　A buddha in the temple shrine

Make yourself a Deva King[10]
    Standing at the gate outside!

If you search for the Pure Land
    Bent upon your own reward
You'll only find yourself despised
    By the Buddha after all!

People have no enemies
    None at all right from the start
You create them all yourself
    Fighting over right and wrong

Clear are the workings of cause and effect
    You become deluded, but don't
          know
It's something that you've done yourself
    That's what's called self-centeredness

Grown used to the conditioned world
    Grown used to the world of
          transience
When you become deluded like this
    You're the one who's losing out!

The mind that's not conditioned
    Is originally unborn
What is conditioned doesn't exist
    That is why there's no delusion

Though the years may creep ahead
    Mind itself can never age
This mind that's
    Always just the same

Wonderful! Marvelous!
    When you've searched and found at
          last

The one who never will grow old
—"I alone!"[11]

The Pure Land
Where one communes at peace
Is here and now, it's not remote
Millions and millions of leagues
away

When someone tosses you a tea bowl
—Catch it!
Catch it nimbly with soft cotton
With the cotton of your skillful
mind![12]
(*zenshū*, pp. 519–522.)

LETTERS

(The following letter from Bankei's original teacher Umpo (1572–1653), together with Bankei's reply, was reportedly written while Bankei was studying under Umpo's heir Bokuō at the Sanyūji in Bizen.)

Having the opportunity to send a message, I am writing you this note. I trust you are keeping well. I myself am the same as ever, while the good people of Kariya and Nakamura[1] are untiring in their Zen study. As you know, this old monk stands alone on the summit of a solitary peak,[2] and never quotes even a word of the buddhas or patriarchs. However, since you and Akashi[3] have shown an earnest desire, I cannot do other than extend a helping hand and offer you some words of teaching, muddying things up with useless talk.

Now that I have twenty or thirty people coming to the temple to practice zazen, I leave them on their own, and that way everyone feels at ease. If those who use "patriarchal Zen"[4] and forcibly discipline their students were to hear what I'm doing, I'm sure they would consider me the enemy of all the buddhas in the three worlds![5] People may say the bright moon is falling into murky water, but if I can save one student or even half a student, shouldn't I count myself fortunate?

I hope you will be able to return soon.

With sincere regards,
(Umpo)

(Bankei replies:)

Thank you for your letter. Nothing makes me happier than to learn that all is well with you. Everyone here in the temple, from the senior priests to the regular practitioners, is fine, so fortunately there is no need to concern yourself over us. As I learn from your letter, you have lately come down to work shoulder to shoulder with the people of the world in order to save them. This is truly wonderful and praiseworthy.

I plan shortly to come and pay my respects to you.

> With sincere regards,
> (Bankei)
> (zenshū, pp. 319–320.)

(Addressed to Bankei's childhood friend Sasaki Nobutsugu,[6] this letter appears to be the product of a stay in Kyoto circa 1642. School seems to have remained a sore point with the young Bankei, who here professes little enthusiasm for his "academic studies," which may well have included both Buddhist and non-Buddhist classics.)

Twenty-second day of the fifth month (equivalent to late June in the present calendar)

Lately my time has been completely taken up with work, but allow me to address you this brief message. I trust that all is well with you. I myself am fine. I thought this spring[7] I might travel to Edo or perhaps even retire to the mountains; and although I'd already made up my mind to quit my academic studies, everyone said it would be a mistake for me to abandon them now and that at all costs I should go on with my work for another year or so—for the sake of the Dharma, they told me. So, in one way or another, they held me back, and I was obliged to stay on here and keep at my work. I'm doing fine and making good progress, so set your mind at ease. Since I'm already committed to this situation and can't avoid spending another

year or two at my studies, I'd appreciate your putting together some funds to carry me through this period. Next
month I'll have to make my usual journey to Akō to visit
Umpo, so I hope you'll give this matter your immediate
attention. Nothing else in particular to add for now.

> Your servant,
> Yōtaku
> (zenshū, p. 527.)

*(Bankei's disciple Yōsen, to whom this letter is addressed,
was a sister-in-law of Sasaki Nobutsugu. She would have
been about twenty years old in 1656, when the letter was
probably composed, and remained a supporter of Bankei
throughout his career.)*

Allow me to address you this brief message. Concerning your religious practice: as your thoughts haven't yet
stopped, you must make every effort to rouse your faith,
completely forgetting all thoughts, of *every* sort—thoughts
of cherishing good and loathing evil, of loving or hating,
of worldly affairs, of cherishing buddhahood, of loathing
delusion or cherishing enlightenment. If nothing at all
remains in your mind, then your religious practice is complete, so if you can come to this quickly, I'll be able to give
you my acknowledgment. By assiduously rousing your faith,
you'll quickly escape these delusions. When you have escaped them, I'll know it, and at that time I'll be able to
give my acknowledgment to that one who has escaped.

> Respectfully,
> (Bankei)
> (zenshū, pp. 527–528.)

*(The following is a letter from Bankei to his disciple Rintei
(1630–1702), addressed by her earlier religious name Ritei.
Like Yōsen, Rintei was a sister-in-law of Bankei's patron
Sasaki Nobutsugu. She became a nun in 1679, settling in*

a hermitage within the compound of her husband's home.
Bankei's letter was composed sometime before 1691, when
she assumed the name Ritei, and Akao has suggested a date
in the early to mid–1660s.)

Having received your letter, allow me to address you
this brief message. I hope you are all well. I myself am
fine, so please rest assured. You are, I imagine, applying
yourself diligently in your religious practice. Your constant
strong desire to attain enlightenment right away, however,
will make you deluded, so it's essential that you give up
this attitude and just remain without any sort of discrimination or understanding. Don't hate the arising of thoughts
or stop the thoughts that do arise; simply realize that our
original mind, right from the start, is beyond thought, so
that, no matter what, you never get involved with thoughts.
Illuminate original mind, and no other understanding is
necessary. However, if you become [attached to] the desire
for illumination, then it will become a source of delusion.
Only realize that, from the beginning, original mind is
beyond thought, and don't attach to your rising thoughts
at all, whether they're about good or evil, Buddhism or
worldly matters, your own affairs or other people's—whatever they are, just let them arise or cease as they will, and
that way you'll naturally accord with original mind.
Thoughts arise temporarily in response to what you see
and hear; they haven't any real existence of their own. You
must have faith that the original mind that is realized and
that which *realizes* original mind are not different.

Should you have any further questions, don't hesitate
to ask.

Respectfully,
(Bankei)
(*zenshū*, pp. 530–531.)

(This letter, probably dating from the mid–1670s, is ad-
dressed to Lady Naga, daughter of Bankei's samurai patron

*Katō Yasuoki and wife of Lord Katō's chief retainer Ōhashi
Shigeyoshi. Rikyō, who seems to have been an elderly lady-
in-waiting in the Ōhashi family, had apparently sought to
meet with Bankei to receive his guidance on how to confront
her approaching death. Bankei, unable to see Rikyō, passed
on this message to her via Lady Naga. The first part of the
letter deals with unrelated material and has been omitted.)*

. . . On my way back this time, I won't have a chance
to see anyone, so please convey my heartfelt regrets to
Rikyō. Even for one who is young, life is uncertain at best,
so for someone like Rikyō who is well-advanced in years it
is all the more understandable to feel regret. Since I too
am not only old, but ailing as well, it is very unlikely that
I will be able to see her again. Nevertheless, since she is
sincerely committed to the Dharma and is practicing
wholeheartedly, I'm sure she will illuminate the principle
of original buddhahood and become the sort of person who
does not rely on the power of others. So my leaving for the
capital is in no way a cause for such unhappiness on her
part. This Dharma isn't anything you can learn from
someone else. Even if she did see me, it would not help.
Please convey this message to her from me.

Also, it keeps skipping my mind, but as Rikyō is old
and prepared [to meet death] at any time, secure [in her
faith], I think she should be sure to sew herself a seven-
piece *kesa*,[8] so that when death comes she'll be ready with
it. They say: "When you [return] to your native place, deck
yourself out in brocade."[9] Well, there's no amount of brocade that can compare with wearing the *kesa*, so please tell
her when she goes back to her native place to have on a
seven-piece *kesa*. I think it's wonderful that a woman is
able to prepare a *kesa* for herself.

If I go to the capital now, I probably won't have the
chance to see Rikyō again, so please give her this message
from me: At the time of death, there's no need for any
special state of mind. Just meet your end with the ordinary

mind of zazen. Everybody's mind is the Buddha Mind, which is originally enlightened, so it's not something that is "born" or that "dies"; it neither comes nor goes, but is eternal, unalterable buddhahood. Thus, it's not a matter of your *becoming* a buddha now for the first time since you've *been* a buddha right from the start. That's why, instead of following other people's spiritual guidance, it's best to look to your own ordinary straightforward mind. Please tell her this for me. And since it's the same for your Ladyship, and anyone else as well, don't think that this is only for Rikyō.

Respectfully,
Bankei
(*zenshū*, pp. 533–534.)

Instructions for the Layman Gessō, given at his request
(Bankei composed the following instructions on the art of combat for his disciple and patron Katō Yasuoki, daimyo of Ōzu and an expert in the use of the yari, *or Japanese lance. Although not specifically a letter, it has been included here.)*

In performing a movement, if you act with no-mind, the action will spring forth of itself. When your *ki*[10] changes, your physical form changes along with it. When you're carried away by force, that is relying on "self." To have ulterior thoughts is not in accordance with the natural. When you act upon deliberation, you are tied to thought. The opponent can then tell [the direction of] your *ki*. If you [try to] steady yourself by deliberate effort, your *ki* becomes diffuse, and you may grow careless. When you act deliberately, your intuitive response is blocked; and if your intuitive response is blocked, how can the mirror mind appear?[11] When, without thinking and without acting deliberately, you manifest the Unborn, you won't have any fixed form. When you are without fixed form, no opponent will exist for you in the whole land. Not holding on to anything, not relying onesidedly on anything, there is no "you" and no "enemy." Whatever comes, you just respond, with no traces left behind.

Heaven and earth are vast, but outside mind there is nothing to seek. Become deluded, however, and instead this mind becomes your opponent. Apart from mind, there is no art of combat.

(Tomisusanshi, zenshū, p. 940.)

"WORDS AND DEEDS"

(Miscellaneous Materials)

Bankei's childhood

From the time he started his schooling, the Master was occupied studying the Confucian classics at the Daigakuji.[1] This was not to his liking, and he was always returning home early. His elder brother Tadayasu[2] rebuked him for this time and again, but the Master would not listen. On his way home, he had to cross the Ibo River.[3] Tadayasu commanded the ferryman: "If he comes back early, don't take him across on any account!" One day, the Master was returning early, and the ferryman followed Tadayasu's orders. The Master declared: "At the bottom of the river there must be solid ground!" He plunged right to the bottom, and, gasping for breath, managed to gain the opposite bank.

One day, he said to himself: "I have no wish to study the Confucian classics, and when I go back to the house my older brother will only scold me again. Better for me to die—why should I cling to life?" Thereupon, he swallowed some poison spiders which were known to be absolutely lethal to men, filling his mouth with them, and, secluding himself in a small stone shrine,[4] quietly awaited death. However, his luck still had not run out, and when dawn arrived, he emerged again.

On the fifth day of the fifth month it was the time-honored custom for all the local boys to divide into teams that were spread out along the opposite banks of the river, letting fly a hail of pebbles to see which side would win. If the Master were on one side, his opponents on the opposite bank would scatter to escape his attack. He would never retreat until victory was his.

(*Itsujijō, zenshū*, p. 411.)

The priest's Fudō

The Fudō Hall [of the Ryōmonji] is situated to the right of the temple gate. During the Kanei era,[5] the abbot Jukin of the nearby Saihōji[6] owned a small statue of Fudō that had been carved by Kūkai.[7] Its length was scarcely four inches, and it was possessed of an exquisite spiritual presence. At this time, the Master was still very young. "How I wish I could have that!" he thought to himself. Jukin, however, prized the image highly and would not part with it.

One day, the Master reflected: "If I pray, surely it will come to me. If my prayers have no effect, then Buddhism isn't worth believing in, and even if I realized [the Dharma], what use would it be?" So, setting aside a period of thirty days, he worshipped with great devotion, praying single-mindedly for divine assistance. But the twenty-ninth day arrived without any result. Evening came, and a friend happened by to visit. During the course of their conversation, the Master explained the reason for his activities, and told his friend straight out that he could not believe in Buddhism. He had scarcely finished speaking when suddenly Jukin came and knocked at the door. The Master was surprised to see him there and greeted him, saying: "Why have you troubled yourself to visit me at this late hour?" Jukin said: "I am going to entrust to you this precious image. I felt a strong urging in the depths of my heart, and so [decided to come] immediately without waiting till morning." He then drew the statue from his robe and gave it to the Master. In the Master's mind, there arose an extraordinary feeling of determination, and he finally resolved to become a monk.

(*Ryōmonji shiryaku, zenshū*, pp. 587–588.)

At the post station

During the Master's *angya*,[8] he passed through the post station at Seki[9] in Mino. His feet exhausted, he hired a post horse to ride; but just then a valuable load of merchandise arrived, and the pack horse driver, seized with greed, pulled the Master rudely from the saddle and, setting the load of goods on top, went off. The Master sat down cross-legged beneath the eaves of the station, looking somewhat despondent. Attempting to console him, the dispatcher approached and said: "Monk, are you angry?"

The Master replied: "For the sake of the One Great Matter[10] I went against my parents' wishes, left my native place. And now I've got upset over one trifling thing! How I repent it!" He then rose and left.

"From that moment on," the Master used to say, "I severed the roots of anger."

Afterward, when the Master was teaching, whenever he passed through this post station all the local people would flock to pay him homage. At the station was a man named Seishitchi,[11] who erected a hut for the Master and welcomed him there with offerings. Its traces remain to this day. . . .

(*Itsujijō, zenshū*, p. 419.)

Bankei faces death

When the Master was on *angya*, he boarded a ferry at the town of Yamada in Ōmi.[12] No other passengers were aboard. The boatman steered the ferry to the riverbank, and began to load on stacks of firewood. His movements were furtive, like a thief's. The Master said: "Did you pay for that?" The boatman muttered: "Monk!" "Are you stealing it?" the Master asked. "Shut up!" the boatman told him. The Master said: "If you're going to steal it, then kill me and steal it, but I can't allow you to be a thief." And so saying, he stopped the boatman, prepared to die if necessary.

Ignorant though the fellow was, he yielded to reason, and, unable in the end to carry out his intention, pushed off the boat. . . .

(Itsujijō, zenshū, p. 417.)

Among the beggars

On his return from Kaga,[13] the Master passed through Edo. Stopping at the Komagata shrine,[14] he mingled with the throngs of beggars, cultivating his mind and disciplining himself in religious practice as he nurtured his enlightenment. It happened at that time that the officer in charge of Lord Matsuura Shigenobu's[15] stables was leading a horse, when it broke away. The horse charged through the streets, and crowds of people scrambled to stop it, but without success. Seeing this, the Master remarked: "The reason that horse won't be held is simply that the man and the horse are separate."

On his return, the officer reported these words to Lord Matsuura, who said: "I hear that Yōtaku[16] has come to these parts. Who else but he could have uttered these words!"

He promptly sent someone who knew the Master to investigate, and, just as he had expected, it was he. [Lord Matsuura] then invited the Master to his mansion, and, erecting the Kōtō-an,[17] installed him there. . . .

(Itsujijō, zenshū, pp. 417–418.)

The missing coins

At one time, the Zen Master Bankei was living in cruelly straitened circumstances at Seki-no-yama, in Mino.[18] The villagers thereabouts, moved by his destitute condition, came to his aid and found him lodgings. At that time, the village headman discovered he was missing some ten *ryō*[19] from his money purse and immediately suspected Bankei of the theft. [Thereafter, assistance to Bankei] began to dwindle away.

Over a year passed, when, visiting the home of his son-in-law, the headman found that the missing money had been stolen in desperation by a woman. He then summoned Bankei and explained what had happened, expressing repentance and offering his apologies. Bankei calmly replied: "Very good, very good. However, this had nothing to do with *me*. Whether it was your suspecting me or my being under suspicion—right from the start, there was nothing to it. The whole thing just arose from notions."

(*Zoku kinsei sōgo, zenshū,* p. 477.)

The Confucians

When the Master was visiting the Sanyūji in Bizen, all the local Confucians opposed Buddhism. They abominated the Master's religious name and sought to humiliate him, coming to see the Master and debating with him for nearly three months.

At the conclusion of the debate, their ringleader, a certain Nakagawa, ended by calling Śākyamuni a parasite on the world.

The Master asked: "How is it according to the Confucians?"

[Nakagawa] replied: "Order the kingdom and instruct the people."

The Master said: "I have heard that he who would illuminate the Bright Virtue in the kingdom should first put his [own] household in order. He who would put his household in order should first cultivate himself. He who would cultivate himself, should first straighten his mind. He who would straighten his mind should first make his intention sincere.[20] Now, in your case, what sort of intention is it you're seeking to make sincere, and with what mind are you doing this?"

The fellow was dumbfounded. The Master laughed and said: "If you haven't yet understood the writings of [the sage of] Ro[21] in the east, how can you possibly grasp the meaning of [Bodhidharma's] coming from the *west*?"[22]

[Nakagawa], totally flustered, withdrew.

Thereupon, each of the Confucians, bringing with him his disciples, came to study Buddhism with the Master, even attending the Master's zazen practice.

One of them presented the Master with a poem:

> "The kite soars through the sky
> The fish sports in the sea—"
> The Patriarchs' Zen![23]

The Master said: "How about your *own* Zen?"
The Confucian could not reply.
(Tomisusanshi, goroku, p. 139.)

The rich man's wife

For certain reasons, the Master broke off relations with his elder brother Tadayasu. Tadayasu was on close terms with my great-grandfather Sukeyasu,[24] and the two were just like relatives. Sukeyasu constructed a hermitage on the mountain above our family home, and, inviting the

Master, had him settle there. Here, the Master had a place where he could carry on his meditation practice. The Master himself wrote out the name of the hermitage and placed it outside the entrance. Thus, he was a frequent visitor at our family home, which was just like his own house. After he became a priest, my family would often arrange vegetarian feasts and invite him.

The wife of a certain rich man from Ikaba in Shisō[25]— whose name cannot be revealed here—was possessed by vicious greed and would take any advantage of others in her craving for wealth. Her appearance was like that of a yaksha.[26] Her family remonstrated with her over this, but failed to sway her. All of them urged her repeatedly to attend the Master's sermons, and finally she gave in and set off for Aboshi.

That day the Master had accepted an invitation to a vegetarian feast at our family home, and when the feast had ended, he delivered a public sermon. This woman came and joined the meeting, listening reverently. The sermon had not yet finished when her expression grew soft and gentle, and it seemed as if she were a different person. Before the close of the sermon, she had transformed herself and become a buddha. She tearfully expressed her contrition, and the sins of her past melted away like frost and dew. She immediately had her name entered in the temple register, becoming a nun and living as one the rest of her days. In the devout remainder of her life, she has built herself a simple retreat, making offerings to the monks and nuns and remaining active to this day.

My grandparents, my nursemaid and others personally witnessed these things and never tired of repeating them to me. "The Master's room was narrow," they declared, "but it was no different from the [site of the] sermon at the Vulture Peak!"[27]

(*Itsujijō, zenshū*, p. 415.)

The wolf

Toward evening, the Master was returning to Aboshi from Shisō. A wolf stood in the roadway, and, spreading its jaws, confronted the Master. Looking into the wolf's mouth, he saw that a large bone had become lodged in its throat, and, inserting his hand, removed it. Overjoyed, the wolf submissively drooped its ears, wagged its tail and scurried off. Thereafter, when the Master traveled on this road, the wolf would always come and escort him to wherever he was going. . . .

(Itsujijō, zenshū, p. 416.)

The steward's invitation

When the Master was in Ōzu, he received an invitation from a certain Fujioka,[28] a minor official in the Stores Department. The date had been set, but on the day in question, another invitation arrived, this time from the daimyo of the province. The Master excused himself on account of his previous engagement. People were afraid of the daimyo's [reaction]. But the Master said: "How can I divide my mind between high and low? Isn't this all the more so when a minor official has invited me? For days now he's been anxiously concerning himself about this, personally seeing to the cooking and cleaning and other preparations. His intentions reveal a deep kindness. The daimyo can manage [such things] at a moment's notice, so why does it have to be just today?"

When the daimyo learned of these words, he was greatly impressed. The words were the Master's, the admiration, the daimyo's. The daimyo was his Lordship Katō Yasuoki, a great man and a past master of the military arts, before whom even Yui Shōsetsu[29] stood in awe.

(Itsujijō, zenshū, pp. 438–439.)

Heaven and hell

Once the Master was asked by a monk: "Your Reverence always teaches that the worlds of paradise, heaven and hell, hungry ghosts and fighting demons are all in the mind and don't exist outside, etc. But in the Sutra, [the Buddha] says that if you travel westward across a billion buddha lands, there's a region called Paradise, which is the manifestation of the Buddha Amida.[30] Does that mean the Buddha is lying?"

The Master said: "Who decided on that direction?"

(*Zeigo, zenshū*, p. 298.)

From your own mouth

A certain fellow asked about the words of the old masters.

The Master said: "Understanding one phrase, puzzling over another, [and so on for] ten million words—there's never an end to it. If you truly realize what I'm teaching, then from your own mouth wonderful words and marvelous phrases will come forth. Otherwise, what use are such things in [studying] the Way?"

(*Tomisusanshi, goroku*, p. 138.)

Genshin's thousand buddhas

The Master visited Katada[31] and paid his respects at the "thousand buddha" altar.[32] The buddhas were carved by the High Priest Genshin of the Eshinin.[33] [The people of] this area gained their livelihood by fishing. Genshin began by erecting a hall and placing within it an image of Buddha. He instructed the people, saying: "If all of you repeat [the name of] Amida[34] with your mouths, then when you haul in the nets with your *hands* you'll be sure to get plenty of fish." Now, even after all this time, things have remained unchanged, and this has become a local custom. When the Master returned to Yamashina,[35] he said: "Genshin had the tremendous compassion of an Icchantika bodhisattva.[36] He is truly worthy of admiration." Everyone exclaimed: "The Master is indeed a kindred spirit of Genshin born into another age!"

I have heard that at Kawachi[37] there are seven cremation grounds established by Gyōgi Bosatsu.[38] All four sides as well as the rocks [covering] the ground are carved with buddhas and dharani.[39] Gyōgi's last words were: "Anyone who receives cremation in these recesses, even those who have committed the five cardinal crimes and the ten evil acts,[40] will be sure of reaching heaven and becoming a buddha." This sort of enlightened activity and magnificent compassion is just like that of Genshin.

Now we come to the phony teachers of Zen who are in fashion these days. When they hold forth on the records of the patriarchs, they abuse the buddhas and patriarchs, disdain the old worthies. Then they try to play upon the feelings of ignorant laymen, carrying on about the eight hot and cold hells,[41] weeping right along with their audience and striking terror in their hearts. Or else they chatter about going to heaven and becoming buddhas and seduce their listeners [with talk of] the excellent rewards of accumulating merit, just like an actor cajoling a foolish child. But when you take a good look at what's really on their minds, it's all grubbing donations and making a name for themselves. If anyone questions this, they say: "This is a skillful expedient [for teaching Buddhism]." The truth is, they themselves become guides on the road to hell, pulling down the ignorant masses. How pitiful they are!

(*Itsujijō, zenshū,* p. 448.)

Offerings

The Master was going to send a shrine offering[42] and, ordering fifty wax candles, had them placed in a box. The box was large, [but] when the Master opened it and looked inside, [he saw that] the bottom had been thickly spread with straw. He ordered this to be removed and then put in an additional fifty candles, filling up [the box].

He said: "Offerings are the true expression of sincerity. To indulge ostentatiously in empty show, to delight in false display, is utterly contrary to the intent of this old monk. From here on, you are never to do this!"

Nowadays at funeral services they pile high the offerings, in the meantime filling up the bottom by tying together [bundles of] straw. Then they crown it all with gorgeous flowers and ask the director of the service to come and look. Even if another service is scheduled, they just go ahead and hold it without changing anything. They may go on like this for ten or even up to a hundred [services], until [the offerings] change color and start to disintegrate. Only then do they put in fresh ones!

Confucius reviled those who made grave figures.[43] But this business now is still worse. Among the Master's followers, this is something that's never done. As a rule, whether it was the [anniversary of] the buddhas or the patriarchs or that of an ordinary deceased, whenever he attended the ritual meal accompanying a service,[44] [the Master] would be sure the ceremonial vessels were filled and the offerings fresh. On such occasions he made no distinction between the food for the living and that offered [the deceased]. . . .

(*Itsujijō, zenshū*, pp. 435–436.)

Counting

The attendant monk Jin asked: "In the past when your Reverence was single-mindedly practicing zazen, how many sticks of incense would you burn for the day and night?"

The Master said: "When I was sitting the whole day through, I didn't count the number of sticks of incense. I just considered one stick of incense as one day, and one stick of incense as one night."

Jin, in spite of himself, was left dumbfounded.

(*Tomisusanshi, goroku,* p. 139.)

Soen's special teaching

Among the Master's disciples was the monk Soen.[45] His character was plain and true, independent, firm, dignified, and in his behavior no one could discern a single flaw. On the battleground of Dharma he was a valiant and accomplished hero. Yet the Master always admonished him for his aggressive outspokenness. Soen tended to thrust himself to the fore, and the Master would rebuke him and push him back. This only made Soen all the more determined to force his way to the front. Finally, he was expelled. Time and again he would return, expressing his contrition and rejoining the assembly. This occurred on several occasions. No one understood the reason for [the Master's actions], but people speculated that he might be trying to temper the harshness [of Soen's character], continually shuffling him this way and that as a compassionate means of instruction.

During the Great Training Period held at the Ryōmonji in the third year of Genroku, Soen became ill and was on the point of death. The Master [visited him] in the *enjūdō*[46] and spoke to him intimately, saying: "*Ajari,*[47] each day you live is a day to work for others."

Soen nodded and passed away.

The others had never realized how great was the compassion of the Master's words.

(*Zeigo, zenshū,* p. 305.)

Positive and negative

A monk of the Shingon school questioned the Master: "In my school's meditation on the letter *a*,[48] there are two methods of meditation on the Unborn: the negative and the positive. Isn't this positive method what your Reverence is teaching?"

The Master said: "Come over here."

The monk approached him.

The Master shouted: "Which method is *this*?"

The monk was utterly dumbfounded. The entire assembly was present and heard this, filled with amazement.

(*Zeigo, zenshū*, p. 285.)

Layman Gessō's runny nose

Whenever the Layman Gessō got angry, his nose would start to run. He once asked the Master about this. The master told him: "Is snot any different from tears?"

Thereafter, the Layman did not reveal in his demeanor whether he was pleased or angered.[49]

(*Tomisusanshi, goroku*, p. 138.)

The thief

Among the multitude who arrived to attend the training period was a certain monk from Mino who was known to be a thief. Wherever he went he disrupted the assembly. There were seven or eight monks from the same area who were well acquainted with this and appealed to the local government official, saying: "This monk is an evildoer, known to people everywhere. Have someone get him to withdraw at once and nip this evil in the bud!"

The official reported this to Sekimon, who conveyed the official's words to the Master.

The Master flushed with anger and declared: "At this time I'm conducting a training period at [people's] request—and why do you suppose I'm doing this? It's to alter the evil ways of evil men, to encourage the virtues of virtuous men, so that each person may thoroughly realize his wisdom body. To praise the upright and reject the wayward now would be totally opposed to my real purpose."

Sekimon was speechless, filled with shame and remorse.

Word of the affair was bruited through the assembly, and all shed tears, moved by the [Master's] deep compassion. At that time, the monk in question raised his voice and sorrowfully proclaimed: "Today I have received the compassion of a great teacher! From here on forever after I will cut off evil thoughts and devote myself to cultivating enlightened activity."

Thereafter, wherever he went, in whatever assembly he found himself, he was always known for his diligence.

With the masters of Dharma nowadays, when a student isn't to their liking, they painstakingly search for some tiny fault and then, even if he's their own brother, turn him out without any warning just as if he'd been their worst enemy! On the other hand, if it's someone who will be useful in promoting their own fame and fortune, even if he's from a different line, they'll embrace him and bring him right in, congratulating themselves on their cleverness. Without the mind of compassion, one will be arrogant as a demon or a yaksha. [This sort of thing] is to be firmly rejected and abhorred! Though I[50] have been abbot at Ryōzan[51] for more than twenty years, I have never taken it upon myself to tyrannize the students, for the Master's admonition still rings in my ears. . . .

(*Itsujijō, zenshū*, pp. 433–434.)

Bankei and the stingy monk

Among the Master's disciples was the monk Tsuyō.[52] He was a very meticulous fellow, but was excessively attached to trivial activities, picking up the remains of rice in the hulling room and gathering any greens he found floating in the stream. The Master forbade him to do this. Tsuyō tended to scour the store rooms and corridors for things, and there was nowhere he didn't go. [In the end,] the Master expelled him. Tsuyō asked Tairyō[53] to intercede for him and expressed his contrition, but though years passed, the Master would not pardon him. Finally, begging forgiveness, Tsuyō was readmitted to the assembly. He came and prostrated himself before the Master. The Master smiled and said: "I haven't seen you in quite a while. My, you've been getting old!" Everyone was greatly impressed with the excellence of the Master's compassion.

On reflection, one can see that, because of Tsuyō's failings, the Master was instructing him, and that, throughout, his compassionate attitude had never changed.

(*Zeigo, zenshū*, p. 318.)

The samurai's fan

When the Master was at the Kōrinji, a samurai came to see him. Holding up his fan, the samurai said: "When it appears in the realm of being, this object is called a fan; yet originally it's non-existent. Do you know what sort of thing it is at the moment it descends from Heaven?"[54]

The Master said: "I know."

The samurai asked: "What do you know?"

The Master told him: "I know that I don't know."

The samurai sighed admiringly, and declared: "The Great Sage himself said that 'Knowledge is to say you do not know a thing when you do not know it.' "[55]

The Master shook his head and said: "That's not it at all."

(*Zeigo, zenshū*, p. 311.)

Bankei's "no rules"

In the winter of the third year of Genroku, the Master held a training period at the Ryōmonji. Over ten thousand people attended. Everyone said: "At this meeting they'll surely have to set up rules and regulations, exhort people in a booming voice and make the whole assembly quake with fear!"

But everyone was calm and quiet, and no rules or regulations were imposed.

Periodically, the Master would ascend the lecture seat and address the assembly, saying: "The originally existing Unborn—all of you, be sure you don't conceal it from yourselves! This Unborn is like a great ball of fire: touch it and you'll be burned. I can speak about it for you now, but my words can't exhaust it; I can use it, but I'll never use it up. For me to exhort people, berating them harshly to frighten them into activity, is just a useless deception. It should never be done!"

When the monks of the assembly heard this, all their doubts melted instantly away.

(*Zeigo, zenshū*, p. 296.)

Chōkei's seven cushions

When the Master was at the Fumonji in Hirado in Hizen, the Zen Master and Abbot of the Kōdaiji in Nagasaki[56] came to see him. In the course of their discussion, the Abbot remarked: "In setting forth your instruction, you teach clearly and directly, cutting off all deluded views and not concerning yourself with religious practice. However, what about the story of Chōkei and the seven cushions [he wore out doing meditation]?"[57]

The Master said: "Your Reverence has got the story wrong. This Chōkei spent twelve years going about studying successively with the Zen Masters Reiun, Seppō and Gensha, wearing out the seven cushions, but in spite of all that, he still hadn't experienced any breakthrough. Then, one day, he rolled up the bamboo blind and suddenly realized enlightenment. At that moment, he composed a verse:

> What a difference! What a difference!
> Rolling up the blind, I see the world.
> If anyone asks me what teaching it is I've grasped
> I'll take my whisk and bash him in the mouth!

Your Reverence, study up on this some more!"

The Abbot, filled with admiration, bowed his head in assent.

(*Zeigo, zenshū*, p. 289.)

The fencing master

The Master was at the Kōrinji. When he ascended the lecture seat, a master of the martial arts approached him and said: "I have been practicing for quite some time. Once I'd grasped the knack of it, my hand responded perfectly to my mind, and ever since, when I confront an opponent, before even taking up my weapon, I've pierced through his very 'bones and marrow.' It's like your Reverence's having the Dharma Eye."

The Master told him: "You've certainly done your utmost in the martial arts. Now, attack *me!*"

The samurai was suddenly at a loss.

The Master said: "I've delivered my blow."

The samurai bowed his head and exclaimed in admiration: "How incredible! Your Reverence's attack is swift as lightning, quick as a spark struck from flint. You have surpassed me. I humbly beg to receive from you the essentials of Zen." More and more, his respect for the Master continued to grow.

Generally, when the Master was in Edo, many samurai from the different schools of fencing would come to meet him. All received the Master's single blow, and there was none who failed to respect and revere him.

(Zeigo, zenshū, pp. 293–294.)

Nanryū's place

When the Master was at the Gyokuryūji in Mino, the Sōtō worthy Nanryū[58] took his fan and, pointing to his place, demanded: "Your Reverence, how come you're passing this place up?"

The Master said: "Well, just what sort of place *is* this?"

Nanryū replied: "Unborn and imperishable."

The Master told him: "You're mistakenly caught up in words and names."

Raising his voice, Nanryū said: "Getting older and older,[59] running to the east, running to the west—why are you going around bewitching lay men and women!"

The Master replied: "When you use an evil eye, evil's what you'll see." Nanryū went off, but after a while he came forward and prostrated himself before the Master, expressing his profound gratitude.

(Zeigo, zenshū, p. 307.)

The rays of light

. . . [At the Great Training Period held at the Ryōmonji,] there was a certain monk who stepped forward and said: "I am chanting the Light Mantra.[60] I practice diligently, night and day, and my body emits rays of light . . . etc."

The Master scolded him, saying: "Those rays of light of yours are nothing but the flames of the evil passions consuming your body!"

The monk meekly withdrew.

(*Zeigo, zenshū*, p. 310.)

As you are is it!

When the Master was at the Nyohōji, he instructed the assembly, saying: "All of you are lucky indeed to have met with a teacher! Without having to wear out your straw sandals, to waste your strength [pursuing] flowers in the sky or [to engage in] difficult and painful practices, you [can] directly enter the true teaching. What good fortune! Don't waste your time!"

A monk who was present said: "All the same, there's just one thing. Suppose, for example, someone wants to go out of the city and across the river: without using a boat, much less even taking a step, he'll never get anywhere."

The Master said: "As you are, right here at this moment, is it. There's no getting anywhere or not getting anywhere. This is what's meant by the teaching of sudden enlightenment. Hesitate and it's lost; waver and it draws further and further away."

(*Zeigo, zenshū*, p. 311.)

Settei's medicine

During the training period [held at the Ryōmonji in the third year of Genroku], there were many sick monks. Several monks were assigned to nurse them under the supervision of Settei.[61] Someone remarked: "These fellows are just lazy, pretending to be sick and getting a quiet rest. They ought to be punished and thrown out of the temple!"

Settei said: "It's because they are weary of the meditation practice that they have come to this. This is indeed a grave illness, and I am treating it with the medicine of patience and compassion. [That way,] the day will surely come when they regain their well-being."

(*Itsujijō, zenshū*, pp. 427–428.)

Shopping for the best

When the Master was at the Jizōji in Yamashina, he sent a monk into the city to buy some fine-quality paper. The monk had the disposition of Confucius' disciple Tzu-kung,[62] and he privately evaluated the pros and cons [of the various papers] before making his purchase and returning. The Master told him: "No good," and sent him back to make his selection again. The monk still would not abandon his attitude, and, painstakingly weighing the merits [of each variety], he once more made his purchase and returned. "Still no good," the Master told him. By the third time this had happened, the monk realized his error and, prostrating himself, expressed his repentance. The Master said: "The first item you brought was fine."

(*Itsujijō, zenshū*, pp. 429–430.)

The Confucian's question

A Confucian asked: "If all the men in the world turned to Buddhism, entering the priesthood and abandoning their wives and children, I'm afraid the human race would cease to exist. What do you think?"

The Master said: "Let's wait until that human race has actually died out, and then I'll tell you."

The fellow meekly withdrew.

(*Tomisusanshi, goroku,* p. 138.)

Waste paper/clean paper

The monk Rōzan[63] was stingy by nature. When, as a youth, he wiped the temple oil lamps, he used scrap paper. Seeing this, the Master said: "Why don't you use clean paper?" Was the Master perhaps taking him to task for his stinginess? Thus, in the temples Rōzan founded, even now they use clean paper to wipe the oil lamps. . . .

When the Master wrote large characters, he spread a clean sheet of paper underneath lest the ink should seep through. If, after [the paper] had been used once, someone [wanted to] use it once more, the Master wouldn't allow it, saying, "Don't use it again, or there may be someone else who will go and do the same."

As a rule, handkerchief paper that had been used once was not used over. [The Master] instructed that it should be disposed of. Even for toilet paper, new [paper] was always used. . . .

(*Itsujijō, zenshū,* p. 447.)

Bankei's natural method

Over thirteen hundred people participated in the [Master's] training periods, not including those monks and laymen from outside the temple who came daily to join the assembly. The participants divided themselves among the halls, where they practiced either zazen or chanting. Without setting up any rules, each person just naturally pursued his own activity, practicing diligently and quietly so that it seemed as if there were no one in the room.

These days, the Zen monasteries everywhere crowd together three or five hundred monks, regulating their schedule down to the minute, restricting their area of movement, virtually binding them hand and foot so that it's just like going into a jail. If anyone commits even the slightest infraction, they beat him and throw him out, never showing the smallest forgiveness. Their prying and bullying are worse than a government official's! The result is that, when the training periods finish, some people become ill, while others find themselves completely debilitated. Thus, the seedling is blasted before it can sprout, causing resentment among teachers and parents.

This, then, is the sort of activity carried out nowadays by those who style themselves experts in the teaching of Zen. Alas! Feckless monks, bending whichever way the winds of fashion blow, unable to rise above the common herd—how pitiful they are! The men of old set up the barrier of death, opened the pit where [students] are buried alive.[64] All these things, without exception, were done with a particular purpose in mind, but now people imitate them blindly in the false hope of producing the same result.[65] If a clumsy workman seizes the adze of the [man of] Ch'u, a lot of people are going to lose the tips of their noses![66]

(*Itsujijō, zenshū*, p. 435.)

Bankei's night sermon

When the Master was in his middle years and staying at the Chikurinken,[67] he delivered a sermon one evening[68] to two or three Zen monks. When his talk was finished, everything became quiet and still. Suddenly, with a shriek, a wild boar sprang from behind a mulberry tree. The Master laughed aloud. The monks were thoroughly startled.

(*Zeigo, zenshū,* p. 307.)

The old tree

The Master erected the Kaiganji[69] on the site of an abandoned temple. While clearing the area, an old pine tree was found to be blocking construction. Everyone wanted to cut it down and remove it. The Master said: "The temple can be set up again [elsewhere, but] this old tree did not easily grow so tall and wide. Let it live and don't cut it down!"

Alas! The true meaning of the Master's love for what is old is not to be understood by clever monks. The worthies of long ago planted pine trees to beautify the temple grounds.[70] As the saying goes: "The charming sights at a Zen temple: old monks and aged trees."

Let descendants in later generations take a lesson from [the Master's] deeds and seek to emulate them!

(*Itsujijō, zenshū,* p. 426.)

Bankei and the blind man

In Harima, in the town of Himeji, was a blind man who by hearing people's voices could discern their innermost thoughts. . . . Once, hearing a man passing along a nearby street, singing as he walked, he remarked: "For someone without his head, he sings well."

The man's wife and servants all laughed. "The mouth is *in* the head," they told him, "so that proves you're wrong!"

"Just wait a while," the blind man said.

Singing again, the man returned. Suddenly there was the sound of a head being cut off. The attacker declared:

"I was going to cut him down before, but I saw he was on a mission for his lord, and so I waited."

This blind man always said: "In people's words of congratulations, there is invariably a trace of sadness. In their expressions of condolence, there is always a note of delight. It's the same with everyone. Yet when I hear Master Bankei's voice, its tone never changes: with gain or loss, blame or praise, high or low, young or old, it's always the same, peaceful and calm. He has surely freed himself from ordinary vulgar mind! . . . ."

(Itsujijō, zenshū, p. 431.)

Hachiroemon

During the Master's middle years, there lived in his native village, amid the dusts of the world, a farmer by the name of Hachiroemon.[71] He was on close terms with the Master and was a regular visitor at the temple. Wildly eccentric in his behavior, he was looked down upon by the local people. Yet the outlandish way he conducted himself with the Master utterly amazed them all.

One day, the Master set out from town, and on his way, the two met. Hachiroemon said: "Your Reverence, where are you off to?" The Master replied: "I'm on my way to your village." Hachiroemon asked: "Aren't you taking medicine for stomach pains?" The Master said: "Yes, I am." Hachiroemon stretched out his palm and said: "I beg you for money to buy medicine." The Master spit into his hand, and they both laughed heartily and went off. Their usual exchanges were of this sort. People were unable to tell just how much Hachiroemon knew.

When the farmer was about to pass away, he pillowed his head in the Master's lap. "I am dying on the battlefield of Dharma," he said, "so I suppose you haven't any sort of word for me." The Master told him: "Just pull down the defender!" Hachiroemon asked: "Your Reverence, do you approve my attainment?" The Master replied: "I find nothing wrong."

Weeping, his wife said: "My husband, you are a buddha! Won't you hurry and redeem my own poor ignorance?"

The farmer told her: "Through all my activities I've manifested it fully, in speech and silence, movement and stillness—there's nowhere I've failed to point out to you this essence of Mind. What can I do if you don't understand?"

(*Zeigo, zenshū*, p. 293.)

NOTES

SERMONS

PART I

1. "Beneficent Enlightened Wisdom," an honorary title bestowed on Bankei by the Imperial Court in 1690.
2. Bankei's headquarters temple, located at his hometown of Aboshi, in present-day Hyōgo Prefecture. It was founded in 1661 by Bankei's childhood friend Sasaki Nobutsugu and his brother Naomori (the reading of the names is uncertain), members of a wealthy merchant family of Aboshi and lifelong supporters of Bankei's activities. Banshū is the *on*, or Chinese-derived reading for the old province of Harima, now included in Hyōgo Prefecture. Though the temple's name is often read Ryūmonji, Ryōmonji is the pronunciation given by the nun Yōshō-in (see below, fn. 67) in a letter, and I have therefore adopted this as being closest to the original reading.
3. Zen temples regularly observe two ninety-day periods of intensive practice known as *kessei* or *ango*, the first in the spring and summer months, the second extending from fall to midwinter. Reference here is to the second of these, the winter retreat or *tō-ango*.
4. 1690 according to the Julian calendar.
5. The roster of monks participating in the training period.
6. The Sōtō and Rinzai schools, founded during the Kamakura period (1192–1333), are the two principal sects of Japanese Zen. Though a Zen master of the Rinzai school, Bankei numbered many Sōtō monks among his followers.
7. Japanese schools of Buddhism outside Zen: The Ritsu school, introduced during the Nara period (646–794), stressed observance of the Vinaya, or Buddhist precepts, the two hundred and fifty

commandments obligatory for monks and nuns; the Shingon, or "mantra" school, was the school of Esoteric Buddhism founded by Kūkai (Kōbō Daishi, 774–835); the Tendai school, founded by Kūkai's contemporary Saichō (767–822), advocated the teachings of the Lotus Sutra, but was also deeply influenced by Esoteric Buddhism. Both the Pure Land (Jōdō) school, founded by Hōnen (1133–1212), and the True Pure Land (Montō) school, founded by his disciple Shinran (1173–1262), are based on belief in the saving grace of the Buddha Amitābha (J: Amida), one of the "eternal" buddhas of the Mahayana pantheon. Because of Amitābha's vow that he will aid all those who call his name to be reborn in the Pure Land, a kind of Buddhist paradise in the western heavens, both sects emphasize sincere repetition of the *nembutsu*, the invocation to Amitābha—*Namu amida butsu!* ("Praise to the Buddha Amitābha!"); the Nichiren school, like the Tendai, gives prime importance to the Lotus Sutra, but combines this with a militant belief in the messianic role of the school's founder, Nichiren (1222–1282).

8. The *hōza* or lecture seat in a Zen temple, generally placed in the *hōdō*, or Dharma hall.

9. Teacher of Men and Devas is one of the ten epithets of the Buddha. Devas are divine beings, and the category includes, among others, virtuous men, sages and bodhisattvas (see below, fn. 51).

10. A title of the Buddha, tathagata signifies a fully awakened being.

11. Another name for the Zen school, implying that it transmits not scriptural teachings but the Buddha Mind itself.

12. That is, the idea of "buddha," of an enlightened being, belongs to the relative world of concepts.

13. See below, fn. 14.

14. A common expression in Buddhism, describing the original, eternal, unalterable nature of ultimate reality, which is not born and does not perish, and which can neither be created nor destroyed.

15–16. According to certain Buddhist theories, the history of the Dharma, the Buddha's teaching, is divided into three periods. In the first, the period of the true teaching following the Buddha's death, the Dharma is perfectly upheld in all respects; in the second, the period of the approximate teaching, only the outward forms of the Dharma are maintained—men practice but no longer have the capacity to realize enlightenment; in the last, the degenerate period of the teaching, which includes the present age, neither practice nor enlightenment remain but only the teaching itself. There are different calculations for the length of each period. Generally, the first is said to last five hundred years, the second, five hundred to two thousand years, and the last, ten thousand years.

17. Another name for the Zen school. A "clear-eyed" man is one who has realized enlightenment.

18. That is, even during the degenerate age.

19. *Hōjōjū,* a synonym for perfect enlightenment.

20. The Ritsu school, mentioned above (see fn. 7).

21. Inspirational Buddhist tales, generally containing supernatural elements.

22. According to traditions probably evolved during the T'ang dynasty (618–906), Zen (CH: Ch'an) is said to have had six Chinese patriarchs.

23. A corruption of the word *jikitotsu,* meaning a monk's robe. The *jittoku* was a half-length robe originally popular in the Heian period (794–1191) among lay Buddhist practitioners and priests living in seclusion. In Bankei's day, it was also adopted by artists, doctors, haiku poets and various other groups whose members shaved their heads without being priests.

24. Umpo Zenshō (1572–1653), Bankei's original teacher. See Introduction, p. xxiv.

25. The Ming Zen Master Tao-che Ch'ao-yüan (J: Dōsha Chōgen, d. 1662). See Introduction, p. xxi. Nan-yüan-shan (J: Naninsan) was the site of Tao-che's original temple, located in present-day Fukien province.

26. For Yin-yüan (J: Ingen), see Introduction, p. xxi. Bankei is probably referring here to Yin-yüan's disciple Mu-an Sheng-t'ao (J: Mokuan Shōtō, 1611–1684), rather than to Yin-yüan himself. Bankei's biography shows he was in Mino at the time of Yin-yüan's arrival in 1654 but had returned to Tao-che's assembly when Mu-an landed at Nagasaki in the following year to join his teacher. Fujimoto suggests the mention of Yin-yüan may have been an error by the editor or copyist. While it is possible that Bankei met Yin-yüan on his second visit to Tao-che in 1655, no firm evidence for this exists, and Bankei may simply have confused the teacher and his disciple in recalling events that had occurred some thirty-five years before. See Fujimoto Tsuchishige, *Bankei kokushi no kenkyū* (Tokyo: Shunjusha, 1971), p. 168.

27. Under the Tokugawa Shogunate, Nagasaki (capital of present-day Nagasaki Prefecture) was the only port of entry for foreigners— limited to Dutch and Chinese nationals—and the only city in which they were permitted to settle and establish businesses.

28. Actually, Sugawara, an adopted name Bankei's father received when he moved to the town of Hamada in present-day Hyōgo Prefecture.
29. A masterless samurai. *Rōnin* were a common phenomenon in this period due to the dislocations following the victory of the Tokugawas in 1600.
30. One of the five large islands that compose the Japanese archipelago. Bankei's father and mother were both originally members of the Miyoshi clan of Awa, an old province included in present-day Tokushima Prefecture.
31. Bankei is speaking at the Ryōmonji in Aboshi. Hamada, where Bankei was born, presently constitutes a district within Aboshi, now a ward of the city of Himeji in Hyōgo Prefecture. In Bankei's day, the three apparently comprised separate communities.
32. Originally a chapter of the Book of Rites (*Li chi*), the *Great Learning* became a cornerstone of the Chu Hsi brand of Sung Neo-Confucianism that constituted a kind of official orthodoxy in Tokugawa Japan. Because it was the shortest and among the easiest of the Confucian texts, students generally began their education with the *Great Learning*. The emphasis was on copying and recopying sections of the work, combined with what was known as *sodoku*, blind repetition and memorization of particular passages, reading off the characters without understanding the meaning of the text.
33. The opening lines of the *Great Learning*. The complete passage reads: "The Way of the Great Learning lies in illuminating the Bright Virtue, in loving the people and abiding in the highest good."
34. That is, the Confucian Classics.
35. Literally, seated meditation. Zazen is practiced in most schools of Buddhism, but is a practice particularly identified with the Zen school.
36. See above, fn. 7. At times, the *nembutsu* has been used by Zen monks as a form of meditation practice.
37. A thin, soft paper produced in Bankei's native province of Harima.
38. The spherical fruit of a large deciduous tree found throughout Japan.
39. By Western reckoning, Bankei was sixty-eight when this sermon was delivered, having experienced the realization he describes at age twenty-five.
40. Bankei's mother, who became a nun with the religious name Myōsetsu, died in 1680 at the age of ninety-one.
41. Umpo. See above, fn. 24.

42. An old province now included in Gifu Prefecture.
43. Gudō Tōshoku (1579–1661), one of the leading Rinzai Zen masters of the early Tokugawa period. Gudō was a member of the same teaching line as Bankei's teacher Umpo, a line that leads to the famous eighteenth-century Zen master Hakuin Ekaku (1685–1769).
44. The old name for Tokyo, which replaced Kyoto as Japan's capital during the Tokugawa period.
45. See above, fn. 2.
46. *Kotsuzui.* The pith or heart of the matter, the inner core of one's being. Here, Bankei implies that the teachers won't be able to judge the true depth of his enlightenment experience.
47. Bankei was in his late sixties when he delivered this sermon and was suffering, as he mentions here, from failing health, possibly a form of pulmonary tuberculosis.
48. This statement recalls a passage in the 14th chapter of the *Chuang Tzu:* " . . . Why all this huffing and puffing, as though you were carrying a big drum and searching for a lost child! The snow goose needs no daily bath to stay white; the crow needs no daily inking to stay black. . . ." (Translated by Burton Watson in *The Complete Works of Chuang Tzu* (New York: Columbia University Press, 1968), p. 163.
49. Spanish and Portuguese missionaries had introduced Christianity to Japan in the mid-sixteenth century. After a brief period of success, however, the new religion aroused the suspicion of the government and was brutally suppressed. Many converts were killed, others apostatized or went into hiding. The Shogunate's determined efforts to root out covert Christians continued throughout the Tokugawa period and assumed something of the character of a witch-hunt.
50. It is unclear precisely what Bankei means by this remark, as he was born in Hamada, the site of the Ryōmonji, where this sermon is being delivered. Forty years previously, in 1650, Bankei had returned to the area after his unsuccessful trip to Mino to consult Gudō Tōshoku. At this time, he restored the hermitage at Nonaka, where he had experienced enlightenment, and "forty years" possibly refers to Bankei's first teaching efforts in his native district, leading to the founding of the Ryōmonji in 1661.
51. Buddhism frequently distinguishes ten different realms of existence. These are (in descending order) the realms of: buddhas— "enlightened ones"; bodhisattvas—potential buddhas, those who aspire to enlightenment, not for their own sake, but so that they may enlighten others; pratyeka buddhas and śrāvakas—classes

of practitioners for whom enlightenment is realized primarily
for oneself and not communicated to others; devas (see above,
fn. 9); men—sentient beings whose acts can determine their
entry into any of the other realms; asuras—fighting spirits, demonic beings drawn from Hindu mythology; beasts—a joyless
state of existence characterized by blind stupidity, a world ruled
entirely by desire and lust where even parents and children will
inflict harm on one another; hungry ghosts—beings condemned by their evil deeds to suffer constant hunger and thirst;
and hell dwellers—the worst offenders, those whose evil deeds
condemn them to lasting torment in any of a series of grotesque
hells said to lie beneath the earth. The first four constitute the
world of enlightenment, transcending the round of death and
rebirth; the remaining six constitute the world of illusion through
which the ignorant are condemned to transmigrate according to
their good or evil karma—the accumulated fruits of their activities in this and previous lives. The last three, considered particularly odious, are known collectively as the Three Evil Paths,
and are often combined with the asuras realm as the Four Evil
Paths. While Bankei's interpretation of the evil realms is often
literal, he frequently treats them as psychological states as much
as objective realities.

52. The *kappa* is an imaginary creature who appears frequently in
    Japanese folklore. He has a face like a tiger, a beak, a body
    covered with scales and on his head a kind of concave saucer
    which, when filled with a small quantity of water, gives him
    tremendous power. He is often said to lurk near bodies of water
    and lure animals, children and unwary travelers to their deaths.
53. A famous brigand of the twelfth century.
54. It was customary for magistrates in Bankei's period to recruit ar-
    rested criminals to serve as spies. Later, the practice was aban-
    doned and regularly employed detectives were used.
55. To commemorate the Buddha's enlightenment, a week-long period
    of intensive meditation practice known as *rōhatsu* is observed in
    Zen temples beginning on the first day of the twelfth month and
    culminating at dawn of the eighth day, when the Buddha is said
    to have experienced awakening on seeing the morning star.
56. For Tao-che (J: Dōsha), see above, fn. 25. As a young monk,
    Bankei had studied under Tao-che at his temple in Nagasaki
    (see Introduction, p. xxv).
57. One of the six supernormal powers or functions of the buddha and
    bodhisattva. The other five are the powers of unlimited vision
    and unlimited hearing and understanding, the power to recall

previous lives, the power to appear anywhere at will, and the power to cut off the stream of transmigration.

58. One of the most famous Zen koans, the story appears in the thirteenth-century collection *Wu-men kuan* (J: *Mumonkan*), "The Gateless Gate." It concerns an old monk who, asked if an enlightened man is subject to birth and death, answered that he was not, and was consequently reborn as a wild fox for five hundred lifetimes. The monk is finally released when the Zen Master Po-chang Huai-hai (J: Hyakujō Ekai, 720–814) gives him the answer that an enlightened man is not *blind* to birth and death. In the Far East, the fox is known for his skill at dissembling, and "wild fox Zen" is a common epithet for those who falsely pretend to have experienced enlightenment.

59. Bankei's caustic remark here recalls a passage in the *Lin-chi lu* (J: *Rinzai roku*. See Introduction, p. xxxv): "... What are you looking for in these lands of dependent transformations! All of these, up to and including the Three Vehicles' twelve divisions of teachings, are just so much wastepaper to wipe off privy filth. . . ." (Translated in R. F. Sasaki, *The Record of Lin-chi* (Kyoto: The Institute for Zen Studies, 1975), p. 21.)

60. The language Bankei uses here refers to the give-and-take of the Zen *mondō* (literally, "questions and answers"), also known as *mondō shōryō*, exchanges in which student and Zen master directly confront one another through words and actions, "testing and weighing" (*shōryō*) one another's understanding.

61. Because they were devised to deal with specific circumstances in the past and are no longer necessarily relevant.

62. The Bodhisattva Avalokiteśvara, the embodiment of compassion toward the sufferings of sentient beings. Bankei's Kannon remains the principal image, or *honzon*, of the Ryōmonji and is one of many Buddhist statues Bankei sculpted during his lifetime. A number of his wood-carving tools are still preserved.

63. The Chinese-derived reading for the old province of Mutsu (present-day Aomori Prefecture).

64. An old province now included in Shimane Prefecture.

65. *Dokusan*, the private interview with a Zen master which is a regular feature of Zen study.

66. A feature of Pure Land Buddhism is the belief that in the present degenerate age man can no longer attain enlightenment through his own efforts at religious practice, termed "self-power"; his only hope is in complete reliance on the "other-power" of Amitābha's saving grace (see above, fn. 7).

67. A preface inserted in the text here reads: "Verbatim notes recording

the sermons of the Zen Master Butchi Kōsai as they were directly preached on the twenty-third day of the eighth month on the occasion of his crossing to the Hōshinji in Marugame, Sanuki, at the close of the eighth month of the third year of Genroku (1690)." Sanuki is the old province that now composes Kagawa Prefecture on the island of Shikoku. The Hōshinji was founded by Yōshō-in (d. 1689), foster mother of Bankei's patron Kyōgoku Takatoyo (1655–1694), the daimyo of Marugame. It was at Yōshō-in's dying request that the sermons recorded here were delivered. Bankei's visit to the Hōshinji, during which these sermons were given, preceded the Ryōmonji training period by about a month; but, whatever the reason, the text has placed the Hōshinji sermons last.

68. The Jizōji, a temple Bankei founded in 1664 in Yamashina, a section of the Higashiyama district of Kyoto. Bankei enjoyed the Jizōji's quiet atmosphere, staying there whenever he was in Kyoto and spending several periods there in retreat. The temple no longer exists.

69. An area in the Higashiyama district where the Tōkaidō, the old highway linking Edo and Kyoto, entered the city.

70. Otherwise unknown. A letter from Lord Kōide to Bankei is preserved at the Ryōmonji.

71. Certain "holy" days set aside by the government during which punishments were suspended.

72. *Raiban*, a platform placed before the temple's main altar. At the beginning and close of his sermon, the teacher mounts the platform and performs a series of prostrations.

73. Shaka is the Japanese pronunciation of Śākya, the shortened form of Śākyamuni, "sage of the Śākyas," the title of the historical Buddha Siddhārtha Gautama (approximate dates: mid-sixth to early fifth centuries B.C.). The Śākyas were the North Indian tribe into which the Buddha was born.

74. An important town of Sanuki province (see above, fn. 67), located some twelve miles east of Marugame.

75. A unit of cosmic time, developed in ancient India. The term kalpa suggests a virtually measureless infinity, the time, for example, in which a universe is born, decays and vanishes.

76. The Buddha Body is the subject of numerous and frequently elaborate theories in Buddhism. Bankei's meaning here, however, seems quite plain: namely, that both sexes intrinsically "embody" the enlightened mind.

77. Ceramic bowls produced in Korea during the Yi dynasty (1392–

1910) were prized in Japan as tea bowls for use in the tea ceremony. Their popularity is said to date from the Regent Hideyoshi's (1536–1598) invasion of Korea, when examples of Korean ceramics first attracted the attention of many Japanese
connoisseurs. As a result, Hideyoshi's Korean campaign (1592–
1598) is sometimes referred to as the "Pottery War." The bowls
Bankei refers to were treasured antiques dating from the sixteenth century.

78. The Kōrinji, one of Bankei's leading temples, erected for him in
1678 in Tokyo's Azabu district by Lord Kyōgoku's foster mother,
the nun Yōshō-in (see above, fn. 67). The Ryōmonji, Kōrinji
and Nyohōji (see below, fn. 80) constituted Bankei's three major
temples. Because of its connection with Lord Kyōgoku's family
and its location in the capital, the Kōrinji was important in
widening Bankei's contacts among the daimyo, or feudal lords,
and their samurai retainers, many of whom became his disciples. The Tokugawa government obliged the daimyo to maintain residences in the capital, where they were expected to live,
generally in alternate years, and where their families remained
as de facto hostages to the Shogunate on their return to their
domains.

79. A familiar practice in the Tokugawa period known as tsujigiri,
literally, "street-corner killing." A samurai anxious to test a new
blade he had acquired would lurk in some deserted spot, waiting
to attack whatever unfortunate pedestrian happened along. By
law, a samurai was permitted to cut down any commoner who
behaved disrespectfully toward him, so that, as in the present
story, the killer might easily concoct some pretext for his attack,
such as the claim that his intended victim had touched his
sword or garments, technically considered capital offenses that
could be punished on the spot.

80. The Nyohōji, in the town of Ōzu (or Ōsu) in Iyo, an old Shikoku
province now included in Ehime Prefecture. The temple was
founded in 1669 by Bankei's patron Katō Yasuoki (1618–1677),
daimyo of Ōzu, then a fief within Iyo province. As seen here,
fiefs are generally named for the castle towns such as Ōzu in
which the daimyo had their principal residences.

81. A ri (CH: li) is approximately two miles; hence, "two or three ri"
here indicates a radius of some four to six miles.

82. Presumably referring to items from the wife's dowry.

83. That is, the husband and the mother-in-law.

84. Magoemon is the merchant's given name.

85. *Namu myōhō rengekyō!* ("Praise to the Sutra of the Lotus of the Wonderful Law!"), an invocation to the Lotus Sutra, recited in the Nichiren school (see above, fn. 7).
86. The four classes that composed Tokugawa society, given in order of importance according to the Confucian-inspired social theory of the period. Note that Buddhist monks and nuns are not included in the categories.
87. The state of perfect oneness and concentration experienced in meditation.
88. A flaming cart that is said to carry sinners to hell and to serve as an instrument of their torment.
89. Judging by Bankei's remarks, the townsman appears to have stayed on after the first lecture to present his question.
90. In Buddhism, clinging, anger and foolishness are often referred to collectively as the Three Poisons, the source of the evils that poison men's minds.

PART II

1. A well-known center for ceramics production in Saga Prefecture on the island of Kyushu. Imari was the ordinary household ware of Bankei's period.
2. See above, Part I, fn. 90.
3. *Kiku*, the set of regulations governing every aspect of the monk's life in the Zen monastery, from his conduct in the meditation hall to the way he removes his sandals. In Rinzai temples today, the *kiku* are generally posted on a board over the back entrance of the monks' hall.
4. In Buddhist temples in China and Japan, the length of meditation is traditionally computed according to the number of sticks of incense burned. A single stick of incense burns for approximately thirty minutes. Hence, Bankei's students had decided to meditate for some six hours a day.
5. In Zen temples, the practice of sitting meditation, or zazen, is punctuated by periods of walking meditation known as *kinhin*.
6. An old Zen expression describing the state in which the student's mind is totally obsessed with a particular problem, so that his whole being *becomes* the problem itself. The "ball of doubt" is often considered the prelude to the experience of *satori*, or enlightenment.
7. See above, Part I, fn. 60.
8. "Chinese words" apparently refers to the Japanese reading of Chinese

Zen expressions traditionally used by Japanese monks in the course of *mondō*.

9. The eye of wisdom, with which the bodhisattva is able to perceive the true state of all things and to save sentient beings.

10. From the standpoint of enlightened mind, the realm of birth and death, of deluded sentient existence, is itself seen to be the unborn and imperishable realm of nirvana.

11. The subject of a popular koan, based on a story told about Hui-neng (638–713), the Sixth Chinese Patriarch of Zen. According to the story, Hui-neng secretly left his teacher's temple after receiving from him the robe and bowl, symbols of the Patriarchal transmission. He was pursued and confronted by a jealous fellow monk, Hui-ming, who was then enlightened when the Sixth Patriarch asked him: "Without thinking of good or evil, right at this moment, what is your original face before your mother and father were born?"

12. Upon entering Buddhism, one vows to take refuge in—to uphold and revere—what are known as the Three Jewels: the Buddha, the Dharma, or the Buddha's teaching, and the Sangha, the brotherhood of adherents.

13. That is, limited to the functioning of the "six senses," considered in Buddhism to be sight, hearing, smell, taste, touch and consciousness.

14. A temple established in 1685 by Bankei's patron Matsuura Shigenobu (1622–1703), daimyo of Hirado, a domain in Hizen province, now included in Nagasaki Prefecture. At Lord Matsuura's request, Bankei became the temple's founder. The present Fumonji is on a different site.

15. That is, some six to eight miles.

16. See above, Part I, fn. 80.

17. A popular koan, often assigned to beginning students. According to the story on which it is based, the Zen Master Chao-chou Ts'ung-shen (J: Jōshū Jūshin, 778–897) was asked by a monk: "Does a dog have buddha-nature?" Chao-chou said: "*Mu!*" (CH: *wu!*) Literally, *mu* means "no," but the koan student is generally urged to concentrate his entire being into the sound itself.

18. Bankei implies that his speaking about the one word "unborn" is as constant for him as the sparrow's chirp and the crow's caw. Elsewhere, he refers more explicitly to the "one word 'unborn.' "

19. By the "world of externals," Bankei refers to all objective existence, including both inner and outer states of being; when perceived dualistically, these are all "outside" the Buddha Mind.

20. That is, when the mind, like water, returns to its original, formless state, it becomes fluid, transparent, with nothing to obstruct its free flow. Bankei thus compares the mind, "frozen" into particular forms, to the water frozen in a tub or container which, when melted, allows the hand to reach in freely and scoop it up.
21. This is similar to a passage in the "Discourses" section of the *Lin-chi lu*: " . . . What do we lack for our manifold activities today? . . ." See Sasaki, *The Record of Rinzai, op. cit.*, p. 8.
22. Sendai was the chief town of Rikuzen Province in northern Japan and is now included in Miyagi Prefecture. In Bankei's day it was part of the old province of Mutsu, of which Ōshū is the Chinese-derived reading.
23. A phrase from "The Return," a well-known poem by the Chinese poet T'ao Ch'ien (371–427).
24–27. The Japanese pronunciation of Bodhidharma, the semi-legendary Indian monk of the sixth century who is said to have brought Zen to China and is traditionally revered as the First Patriarch of Chinese Zen. He is said to have spent nine years in meditation facing a wall at the Shao-lin temple on Mt. Sung in modern Honan. Te-shan Hsüan-chien (J: Tokusan Senkan, 780/2–865) was a specialist in the *Diamond Sutra*, a short Mahayana scripture highly regarded in Zen, but after being enlightened, he burnt all the commentaries he had assembled. Chu-ti (J: Gutei, n.d.) is said to have been enlightened on seeing his master T'ien-lung (J: Tenryū, d. 788) raise a finger, a practice that Chu-ti regularly repeated with his own students. Lin-chi I-hsüan (J: Rinzai Gigen, d. 866) is revered as the founder of the Lin-chi or Rinzai school of Zen. *Katsu!* (CH: *ho!*) is the sound of a shout used by Zen monks. It is particularly associated with Lin-chi, who is frequently described employing it in the *Lin-chi lu*.
28. See Introduction, p. xxxv.
29. An old province now included primarily in the Kyoto municipal district, with some areas included in Hyōgo Prefecture.

HŌGO (Instruction)

1. That is, the Buddha Mind.
2. See *Sermons* (II), fn. 22.
3. Earth, water, fire and wind, which, according to Buddhist theory, are the four physical constituents of the body and of the universe

itself. They represent, respectively, solid and liquid matter, heat and movement.

4. In present-day Ehime Prefecture.

5. Also located in Ehime Prefecture. Nothing more is known of Kantarō.

6. Nothing is known of him.

7. Bankei's disciple Tōgaku Jōsen (d. 1726).

8. Tairyō Sokyō (1638–1688), reputed to have been Bankei's foremost disciple.

9. The remainder of this episode suggests that Jōsen was repeating one of Bankei's familiar statements about the Unborn.

10. Shinran Shōnin (see Sermons (I), fn. 7). Echigo, an old province now included in Niigata Prefecture, was the site of Shinran's five-year exile by the Kamakura Shogunate.

11. "Who is the one who sees and hears?" is a koan that first became popular in Japan during the medieval period.

12. Japanese folk wisdom holds that there are four things to be feared above all others: earthquake, thunder, fire and one's father, in order of fearsomeness.

13. *Sanzen sekai.* Literally, the three "thousand-fold" worlds (SKT: *tri-sāhasra-loka-dhātu*). According to ancient Indian cosmology, the universe consists of three types of interlocking worlds, the lesser, middle and greater, each a thousand times larger than the one preceding it. A thousand of our own universes comprise a single lesser world. In Buddhism, the expression signifies the entire universe and the limitless worlds it contains.

14. The leading temple of the Shingon sect, founded by Kūkai in 816 in what is today Wakayama Prefecture.

15. The headquarters of the Tendai sect, established in 788 by Saichō. Mt. Hiei is northeast of Kyoto, on the boundary between the Kyoto municipal district and Shiga Prefecture.

16. Bankei is referring to the Tōkeiji, a Rinzai temple in Kamakura (Kanagawa Prefecture), founded as a nunnery in 1286 by the widow of the Regent Hōjō Tokimune (1251–1284). Women who wished to escape unhappy marriages could obtain a divorce by taking sanctuary here, even if their husbands followed in hot pursuit. The Tōkeiji is now a temple for monks.

17. Eimyō Zenkō (1653–1716). Originally a Sōtō monk from Ōmi, he became a student of Bankei and eventually the heir of Bankei's disciple Sekimon. Zenkō was the fourth-generation abbot of the Ryōmonji.

18. An old province now included in Shiga Prefecture.

19. Literally, the eighth, or *ālaya* consciousness. The Yogācāra, or

Consciousness Only School of Buddhism, posits eight types of consciousness, of which the eighth is the *ālaya* or storehouse consciousness containing the "seeds" of all thoughts and perceptions. The *ālaya* consciousness is said to be "perfumed" by impressions from outside, and only when these are exhausted does ultimate reality—the pure, unconditioned mind of Suchness—appear.

20. The *katsu!*, referred to previously.

21. Yüan-wu K'o-ch'in (J: Engo Kokugon, 1063–1135) and Ta-hui Tsung-kao (J: Daie Sōkō, 1089–1163), Rinzai masters of the Sung dynasty who were key figures in the development of koan study in Zen. Yüan-wu is known primarily for the koan collection *Blue Cliff Record* (CH: *Pi-yen lu*). His disciple Ta-hui advocated a vigorous, dynamic, non-conceptual approach to koan study, emphasizing particularly the koan *Mu*. The leading lines of Japanese Rinzai Zen today trace their descent from Yüan-wu and his heirs.

22. Bankei's question is rhetorical: "Since the Zen teachers before the Sung dynasty (960–1280) didn't use koans," he asks, "why do I have to?" Although Yüan-wu and Ta-hui were leading early exponents of Koan Zen, the actual use of koans probably predates them. Nevertheless, Bankei is accurate in observing that Koan study represented a later development and was not employed by the majority of masters of the so-called golden age of Chinese Zen in the T'ang (618–906) and Five Dynasties (907–960) periods.

23. Nan-yüeh Huai-chang (J: Nangaku Ejō, 677–744). A disciple of the Sixth Patriarch, referred to previously. The episode mentioned by Bankei appears in the *Ching-te ch'uan-teng lu* (*The Ching-te Era Record of the Transmission of the Lamp*), a collection of Zen biographies completed in 1004.

24. The stole worn over the Buddhist priest's robe. It is draped over the left shoulder and gathered under the right armpit. The *kesa's* color and size may vary according to the sect and the particular occasion for which it is worn.

25. A temple in the village of Hitaki in Gifu Prefecture. Bankei held a training period there in 1692.

26. Otherwise unknown.

27. The Kanzanji is a Rinzai temple, originally located in the city of Osaka and now moved to another site in the Osaka municipal district. Jiton (n.d.) was the disciple of the Kanzanji's abbot Reigan Sokei (d. 1696), who had studied with Bankei under

Dōsha and became his traveling companion afterward. Bankei was a frequent visitor at the temple.

28. In present-day Nara Prefecture.

29. The Ōbaku sect Zen Master Ryūkei Shōsen (1602–1670). Though he served as abbot of the Myōshinji, Ryūkei abandoned his position in the Myōshinji line to become the disciple of the Ming Zen Master Yin-yüan, referred to previously.

30. Bankei's disciple Keiō Soboku (d. 1691).

31. Bokuō Sogyū (d. 1694), successor of Bankei's original teacher Umpo.

32. The Myōshinji. Umpo and his disciples Bokuō and Bankei were members of the Shōtaku-ha, a Myōshinji teaching line founded by the Zen Master Tōyō Eichō (1429–1504). The Myōshinji annually rotated its abbacy among the Zen masters of its principal lines. Bokuō assumed the abbacy in 1671, and Bankei, in 1672.

33. *Jōshōjin*. To dedicate oneself to a life of constant religious practice, abjuring all worldly impurities. In Japan, the expression *shōjin* may refer specifically to the avoidance of meat-eating, and certain Buddhist temples are famous for their *shōjin ryōri*, or vegetarian cuisine.

34. A well-known expression from the *Lin-chi lu*, sometimes translated as "a man of no affairs," or "a man who has nothing to do." It describes the free and easy spirit of the enlightened man, who has no problems, no entanglements, nothing further to seek. Having realized that originally, just as he is is buddha, there is nothing more for him to bother about.

35. Bizen is an old province now included in Okayama Prefecture. In the winter of 1689–1690, Bankei held a brief training period at the Sanyūji, a temple in the town of Okayama in southwestern Bizen.

36. A neighboring province to Bizen, also now included in Okayama Prefecture.

37. Now an area of Okayama city, referred to above.

38. The school of Nichiren, previously mentioned.

39. Referring to Bankei's initial experience of enlightenment in 1647, described in the *Sermons*.

40. Bankei's retreat in Akō, in present-day Hyōgo Prefecture. It was here that Bankei spent two years of grueling practice before realizing enlightenment.

41. The eye which illumines all things.

42. "I" here and in the sections that follow refers to Bankei's heir, Itsuzan Sonin (or Sojin, 1655–1734), the compiler of the *Hōgo*.

43. A quotation from the *Analects*, in which Yen Yüan praises his teacher Confucius.
44. The former religious name of Bankei's disciple Daien Ryōkō (1624–1706).
45. A mountainous district in present-day Nara Prefecture. See Introduction, p. xxvi.
46. Dokushō Shōen (1617–1694), a monk of the Ōbaku school, who became a Dharma heir of Yin-yüan. His temple was located in Saga, west of Kyoto.
47. A Japanese nightingale.

FROM THE GYŌGŌ RYAKKI

1. Fudō (SKT: Acala) is a wrathful Buddhist deity particularly popular in Japan. The Ryōmonji's Fudō Hall was erected in 1676.
2. *Oshō* is a general term of respect for Buddhist monks, similar to "Reverend," but may have the added meaning of teacher or abbot. Sekimon Somin (1642–1696) was a Dharma heir of Bankei who became the third abbot of the Ryōmonji.
3. Tenkyū Shihaku (d. 1722). A disciple of Bankei.
4. A letter of this period (1692) addressed to Bankei from Lord Kyōgoku's wife indicates that Bankei was suffering from pains in the feet which prevented him from standing.
5. That is, Itsuzan Sonin, the compiler of the present work. The others are Bankei's disciples Reigen Shūin (1653–1718) and Taikei Sokaku (d. 1719). These three, sometimes referred to as the "three *jisha* (attendants)," served as Bankei's close attendants during his last years.
6. Located in Hamada, referred to previously.
7. A sub-temple on the grounds of the Nyohōji.
8. This refers to the religious name assigned by a Buddhist priest, who customarily writes out the characters of the name himself. Buddhist names are given to both monks and laymen on particular occasions, such as joining the priesthood or becoming a lay disciple.

POEMS

1. The T'ang dynasty monk Tsung-mi (780–841) divided Zen into five different grades leading from the lowest to the "highest" truth, which consisted in realizing one's original buddhahood.

2. An expression used in Zen to describe the world of enlightenment.
3. The religious name of Bankei's disciple Katō Yasuoki, daimyo of Ōzu. See also Bankei's advice to the Layman Gessō on the art of combat, pp. 138–139.
4. Now the town of Mitsu in Hyōgo Prefecture.
5. The four physical constituents of the body. See *Hōgo*, fn. 3.
6. The *Lotus Sutra* compares the life of sentient beings in the world of delusion to the situation of children at play in a burning house, oblivious to the flames about to consume them.
7. "Self" (J: *mi*) here includes both mind and body.
8. Tathagata. See *Sermons*, Part I, fn. 10. This verse includes a kind of play on words between the expressions ". . . as it was when you came into the world" and "thus-come one" (a literal translation of the term tathagata), which contain the same characters in different order.
9. That is, which are not innate.
10. J: *Niō.* Twin guardian demons of ferocious mien, often placed at the entrance to Buddhist temples in Japan. Bankei implies that rather than trying to become a "shrine buddha" wrapped in sanctity, the student should manifest the dynamic spiritual power symbolized by the Deva Kings. Suzuki Shōsan (1579–1655), another Zen master active during the early Tokugawa period, was known for urging his students to imitate the attitude of the Deva Kings rather than practice a quiet introspective form of meditation. See Introduction, p. xx.
11. That is, original mind is not something that exists outside, but your own true identity. On another level, this implies that, for the enlightened, true self alone remains, with all dualism dissolved, as in the Buddha's supposed pronouncement at birth: "In heaven and on earth, I alone am to be revered!"
12. Bankei is apparently addressing his audience here: "I am passing you my precious teaching," he seems to say; "accept it, don't miss your chance! It is fragile as a rare tea bowl, so receive it with your 'soft,' resilient mind. Receive it stiffly and it will smash and come to nothing."

LETTERS

1. Hamlets in Akō, the site of Umpo's temple, the Zuiōji.
2. Umpo is probably referring to an expression that appears in the *Lin-chi lu*, "The man on the summit of a solitary peak." The actual meaning of this phrase is uncertain, but in Japan it has some-

times been interpreted as a metaphor for the enlightenment of the pratyeka buddha in contrast with that of the Mahayana bodhisattva—the realm of "tathagata Zen" as opposed to that of "patriarchal Zen," referred to below. Umpo's use of these expressions is somewhat ironic, and what he seems to be affirming, above all, is an attitude of determined independence.

3. Unidentified.

4. The term "patriarchal Zen" became popular during the Sung dynasty to describe the method of sudden and complete enlightenment reputedly transmitted by the patriarchs of Zen, beginning with Bodhidharma. This was contrasted with the "gradual" approach of progressively eliminating defilements, which was dubbed "tathagata Zen."

5. The buddhas of the past, the buddhas of the present, and the buddhas who are yet to come, i.e., all enlightened beings.

6. See Introduction, p. xxvii.

7. Following the text in Bankei kokushi no kenkyū, p. 102.

8. A traditional Buddhist death robe made from seven pieces of material.

9. Apparently a popular saying. The actual meaning seems to be that when you go back to your hometown you should put on all your finery—that is, after you've made it, go back to the village and show off; but Bankei has given the expression an interesting twist.

10. Ki (CH: ch'i) is a kind of vital force, the dynamic physical manifestation of mind. The concept of ki remains important in many Chinese and Japanese martial arts.

11. That is, the mirror mind which clearly reflects all things.

"WORDS AND DEEDS"

1. A temple of the Pure Land sect in Bankei's native village of Hamada. Early education for boys in pre-modern Japan frequently occurred at such terakoya, or temple schools, classrooms set up in the local Buddhist temple where young men were taught the basics of reading and writing. Bankei reportedly studied at the Daigakuji together with his friend and future patron Sasaki Nobutsugu, but disliked the course of study and eventually dropped out. See Introduction, pp. xxiii.

2. Tadayasu (d. 1661), Bankei's older brother, had become head of the

family after his father's death, succeeding to his medical practice.
3. A river located in what is now Hyōgo Prefecture.
4. These were traditional stone shrines containing alcoves in which images and gravestones could be placed, the alcoves being frequently large enough to accommodate a person. Bankei's abortive suicide attempt described here was said to have occurred at the family temple, the Hamada Saihōji. Bankei's father was buried at the Saihōji, which had been originally restored by Bankei's middle brother Juden (n.d.), a Pure Land priest. The stone shrine of the story is still preserved at the temple.
5. 1624–1643. Fujimoto suggests the events described here occurred in 1636, when Bankei would have been fourteen.
6. For the Saihōji, see above, fn. 4. Jukin was the teacher of Bankei's middle brother, the Pure Land Priest Juden.
7. See Sermons, Part I, fn. 7. Because of Kūkai's fame in Japan, as both a religious teacher and calligrapher, works of art were frequently attributed to him. According to a legend still current in Bankei's native area, the statue was of Kannon rather than Fudō.
8. Angya, "traveling by foot," is the pilgrimage during which the Zen monk leaves his teacher's temple and travels, practicing Zen and visiting various masters to test and broaden his understanding. See Introduction, p. xxiv.
9. A town in present-day Gifu Prefecture.
10. That is, enlightenment.
11. A pack-driver from Seki who reportedly took Bankei on his unsuccessful journey to visit the Zen Master Gudō in 1648. He subsequently returned with Bankei and erected a hut for his use in Seki's Kitta district.
12. Ōmi is an old province, included in present-day Shiga Prefecture.
13. An old province included in present-day Ishikawa Prefecture.
14. A Buddhist shrine belonging to the Asakusadera, a well-known Tendai temple in Tokyo. Its principal image is a horse-headed Kannon. The episode related here is said to have occurred during Bankei's visit to Edo in 1655, when he was thirty-three. According to contemporary descriptions of Edo, colonies of beggars and other social outcasts had established themselves in the Asakusa and Shinagawa districts of the city. They were formed into a guild of sorts, with a chief for each district who reported in turn to a general commander of all the city's beggars.
15. See Introduction, p. xxvi.

16. That is, Bankei.
17. A hermitage established for Bankei by Lord Matsuura in a suburban mansion that served as his principal headquarters. Lord Matsuura later erected a temple on the site, the Tenshōji.
18. In present-day Gifu Prefecture.
19. An old unit of Japanese coinage.
20. Bankei quotes a passage from the opening of the *Great Learning*.
21. Lu (J: Ro), the state in which Confucius was born, located in present-day Shantung Province.
22. That is, the truth of Zen, which Bodhidharma is said to have carried from India to China.
23. The opening lines of the Confucian's poem derive from the *Mean (Chung-yung)*, which, like the *Great Learning*, was a classic particularly revered by Neo-Confucianism. The verse is said to express the manner in which all living things delight in manifesting their own inborn natures.
24. Nakabori Sukeyasu (n.d.), headman of the village of Shimomura, was an old family friend, having originally assisted Bankei's father in settling in the Aboshi area. See Introduction, p. xxiv. Sukeyasu was the great-grandfather of Daitei Zenkei (d. 1788), compiler of the *Itsujijō*, from which this episode is drawn.
25. Now the town of Yamazaki in Hyōgo Prefecture.
26. A man-eating demon of fearsome aspect.
27. Mount Gṛdhrakūta, where the Buddha is said to have delivered the Lotus Sutra.
28. Fujioka Kenshitchi (n.d.), a minor official serving under Lord Katō. He was assigned to look after Bankei during his visits to Ōzu.
29. A renowned military strategist of the early Tokugawa period. He died in 1651.
30. The monk is quoting a famous passage in the *Amitābha sūtra*, a popular text in Pure Land Buddhism.
31. A town in present-day Shiga Prefecture.
32. A type of altar consisting of multiple Buddhist images grouped together, often miniature images of a particular Buddha, such as Amitābha. The altar in question is a famous attraction of the Jōgōdō, a temple in what is today Ōtsu city in Shiga Prefecture.
33. (942–1017). An early devotee of Pure Land Buddhism. The Eshin-in was the name of his retreat at Yokawa on Mt. Hiei, the headquarters of the Tendai school.
34. That is, the *nembutsu* (see *Sermons*, Part I, fn. 7).
35. The Jizōji, Bankei's temple in Kyoto, mentioned previously.
36. A bodhisattva who himself becomes an *icchantika*, one who is

incapable of realizing enlightenment, in order to save those who are irredeemable.

37. An old province in what is now the Osaka municipal district.

38. (668–749). A popular early Japanese Buddhist practitioner. He was greatly revered by the Emperor Shōmu (r. 724–749), who conferred on him the title "bosatsu," or bodhisattva.

39. Along with mantra (J: *shingon*), dharani constitute the sacred formulas that play an important role in Buddhist practice and ritual. Generally speaking, dharani are longer, mantra shorter, but the expressions are often used synonymously. Although particularly associated with Esoteric Buddhism, mantra and dharani became familiar features of Chinese Buddhism generally. They became popular in Chinese Zen temples during the Sung and Yüan dynasties and similarly found their way into the Zen monasteries in Japan, where many are still included in the liturgy.

40. The five cardinal crimes are patricide, matricide, killing an arhat (a class of enlightened beings), disrupting the harmony of the Sangha, and shedding the blood of a buddha. The ten evil acts are killing, stealing, lechery, lying, being double-tongued, speaking in jest, slander, covetousness, anger and foolishness.

41. Buddhist scriptures describe the tortures endured by sinners condemned to eight hot and eight cold hells.

42. *Nusa*, Shinto offerings, generally made of rope, cloth or paper. In this case, Bankei is apparently sending a gift of candles to a local shrine.

43. Figures buried with the dead. In the *Mencius*, Confucius is quoted as saying that the use of these figures led to the pernicious practice of burying alive retainers to accompany their deceased lord to the grave.

44. *Toki*, the meal offered to Buddhist monks on the occasion of a funeral service.

45. A close disciple of Bankei, Yūhō Soen died during the early part of the Ryōmonji training period of 1690, at which this sermon was delivered. His age at death is unknown.

46. The hospital quarters for sick monks in a Zen temple.

47. The Japanese pronunciation of the Sanskrit word *acarya*, meaning teacher or master. In Zen, it is often used simply as a respectful term of address for monks.

48. In Shingon Buddhism, the letter *a* symbolizes the eternal underlying reality of the universe, personified as the cosmic Buddha Mahāvairocana. This is expressed in the formula *ajihompushō*, "[That which is symbolized by] the letter *a* is originally unborn."

49. Gessō was the religious name of Bankei's samurai patron Katō Yasuoki, mentioned previously. Bankei's reply seems to suggest that for a samurai like Lord Katō, it was as unseemly to give way publicly to anger as to tears.

50. The editor of the *Itsujijō*, Daitei Zenkei.

51. Ryōzan is the "mountain name" for the Saishōji, Daitei's temple in Edo.

52. A former student of Tao-che who later became Bankei's disciple. His dates are unknown.

53. Tairyō Sokyō (1638–1688), reputed to have been Bankei's foremost disciple.

54. That is, at the moment it emerges from the undifferentiated absolute into the world of form. The language of the samurai's question suggests the metaphysics of Neo-Confucianism, which was frequently taking the offensive against Buddhism, and particularly Zen, at this time.

55. A quotation from the *Analects*. "Confucius said: 'Yu, shall I teach you what knowledge is? To say that you know a thing when you do know it and say that you do not know a thing when you do not know it—this is knowledge." Yu was Confucius' pupil, also known as Tzu-lu (542–480 B.C.).

56. Probably Jingen Jishō (d. 1689), sixth-generation abbot of the Kōdaiji, a Sōtō temple in Nagasaki.

57. Ch'ang-ch'ing Hui-lung (J: Chōkei Eryō, 854–932). Becoming a monk at age thirteen, he studied under Ling-yun Hui-tsung (J: Reiun Eshū, n.d.) and subsequently visited the Zen Master Hsüeh-feng I-ts'un (J: Seppō Gison, 822–908) and Hsüeh-feng's heir Hsüan-sha Shih-pei (Gensha Shibi, 835–908). Despite all his studies, however, he failed to resolve his questions about Zen. Even after many years of effort and wearing out seven meditation cushions, understanding still eluded him till, suddenly, raising a bamboo shade, he experienced enlightenment and succeeded to Hsüeh-feng's teaching.

58. Unidentified.

59. Apparently referring to a passage in the *Chao-chou lu*, the record of the T'ang dynasty Zen Master Chao-chou Ts'ung-shen, referred to previously. "Shu-yü remarked: 'Getting older and older— why don't you find a place to settle down?' Chao-chou asked: 'Where can I settle down?' Shu-yü said: 'Getting older and older and he doesn't even know where to settle down!' "

60. The monk is probably a follower of the Shingon school, which is especially associated with the Light Mantra. Practice of the

mantra is said to endow one with a mystical radiance capable of dispelling all evils and obstructions.

61. Bankei's disciple Settei Kiryū (d. 1701).
62. Tzu-kung (c. 520–450 B.C.) is said to have continually compared the relative merits of persons or of things.
63. Rōzan Genni (d. 1740). He studied under Bankei and later became a Zen master in Bankei's line.
64. These expressions apparently express the dramatic character of the demands that the Zen teacher places on his students as he destroys the deluded self. The expression "burying alive" appears in the *Lin-chi lu*. "Everywhere else they use cremation," exclaims Lin-chi, "but here I bury them alive all at once!" (Sasaki, *op. cit.*, p. 29). In Japan, the Sōtō Master Tsūgen Jakuryō (1322–1391) is said to have had a pit dug at the entrance to the monks' hall before which he would examine students seeking admission to the temple. Those unable to reply he would hurl into the pit, which became known as the "pit where men are buried alive."
65. Hsiao p'in (J: kōhin), "To imitate the knitting of the brows." A Chinese expression referring to Hsi Shih, a famous beauty of the sixth century B.C. who, when ill, knit her brows, enhancing the charm of her face and inspiring the homely women of the village to imitate her in the false hope of making themselves beautiful as well.
66. Referring to a story in the 24th chapter of the *Chuang Tzu*. Chuang Tzu tells of a certain plasterer who, finding a speck of plaster on the tip of his nose, would summon his friend, Carpenter Shih, and have him remove it with successive strokes of his adze, an operation which Shih performed without leaving so much as a scratch on the plasterer's nose.
67. A hermitage within the grounds of the Ryōmonji. Bankei took up quarters there during the original construction of the temple.
68. *Yawa*. An evening lecture delivered by the teacher at a Zen temple.
69. A now defunct temple founded by Bankei in what is presently the town of Mitsu in Hyōgo Prefecture.
70. Referring to a passage in the *Lin-chi lu*. Seeing Lin-chi planting pine trees, his teacher Huang-po asked him: "Why plant all those pines deep in the mountains?" Lin-chi said: "First of all, to provide the temple with a nice setting; secondly, to provide a model for later generations."
71. Nothing is known of Hachiroemon.

Translator's Notes

SERMONS

Apart from occasional letters and a small number of poems, Bankei himself wrote almost nothing in the entire course of his career. The sermons provide virtually our only first-hand knowledge of Bankei's Zen. The Master, however, reportedly forbade his disciples to record his teachings, and of the many sermons he delivered, only a small portion survive. These consist primarily of two sets of sermons from the year 1690: a series of talks delivered in early autumn at the Marugame Hōshinji, and portions of another series of lectures from the *dai kessei*, or Great Training Period, held that winter at the Ryōmonji in Bankei's hometown of Aboshi. For the most part, then, what remains to us is one segment of the sermons Bankei delivered during one year toward the close of his life.

Various transcripts of the sermons exist, but in general we know nothing of their authors' identities or of the circumstances in which they were recorded. The sole exception is the so-called Miura MS, a transcript of the Hōshinji sermons by one Miura Tokuzaemon, an otherwise unknown samurai retainer of Bankei's patron Kyōgoku Takatoyo, the lord of Marugame. According to the foreword to the manuscript, Miura attended Bankei's sermons at the Hōshinji on behalf of his aged mother, who was bedridden with illness. Interrupting his regular duties at the castle, he beseeched the temple's priests to allow him a place close to the Master and came faithfully each day to make a record of Bankei's talks, which he then passed on to his mother. Overall, variations exist among the different manuscripts, but most, like the Miura text, appear to be genuine verbatim notes of Bankei's sermons, supplemented at times by reconstructions of his talks and of his dialogues with individuals who approached him during the assemblies.

The sermons have been grouped in two parts, following the Akao and Fujimoto editions, which form the basis for the present translation. Part I consists of two sections, the first recording sermons delivered at the Ryōmonji during the Great Training Period of 1690, the second, sermons delivered at Marugame in the same year. Part II contains materials derived from a manuscript in the possession of the Futetsu-an, a convent established near the Ryōmonji by Ryōun Jōkan (1633–1698), a former haiku poet who became Bankei's leading female disciple. The sermons in Part II are often quite distinct from those in any of the other Bankei manuscripts, and it has been suggested that they were not delivered on the same occasions as the lecturers in Part I. It is possible, however, that they too belong to the talks delivered at the Ryōmonji in 1690. In her dairy, Jōkan notes that Bankei delivered some sixty sermons at the 1690 training period, and it seems natural to assume that different people recorded sermons delivered on different days, accounting for the variety of sermons in the collections.

For convenience sake, selections follow the divisions of the texts given by Akao, but it should be borne in mind that such divisions are assigned by the various editors and are absent from the original manuscripts. Certain portions of the text stand out as discrete and coherent units, but at times it is unclear whether a particular passage represents a continuation of the material preceding it or is merely an isolated fragment, drawn from the same sermon or from some other sermon. Ellipses of three dots at the opening of selections indicate that foregoing material has been omitted; ellipses of four dots at the close of selections or paragraphs indicate that succeeding material has been omitted. Where entire sections from the Akao text have been removed, three asterisks appear at the close of selections. Although a complete translation of both the *Sermons* and the *Hōgo* had been prepared, considerations of space and cost prevented publication of the entire manuscript, and it was thought best to concentrate on particular selections. The captions supplied for these and other materials throughout the book are my own.

In the Tokugawa period, only one collection of Bankei's sermons was published, appearing in 1758. This text provided the basis for the version of the sermons edited by D. T. Suzuki in 1942 for the *Iwanami bunkō* series, but because it contained certain problems, the Iwanami text has since been superseded by two editions of the sermons based largely on manuscripts preserved in the temples founded by Bankei. These appear in the aforementioned *Bankei zenji hōgoshū*, edited by Fujimoto Tsuchishige, and the *Bankei zenji zenshū*, edited by Akao Ryūji. The Fujimoto and Akao texts are very similar, and the present translation makes use of both, as well as of the *Genshiken ganmoku-kan*, a separate sermon text included by Fujimoto. Page references to the texts used for each selection appear on page 193. In every case, the choice of text was determined by a judgment of which version seemed most natural and most in keeping with Bankei's regular speaking style. However, as the Akao text contains frequent interpolations from a wide variety of Bankei manuscripts, as well as certain items not found in the Fujimoto work, I have generally followed the sequence of materials in the *Bankei zenji zenshū*.

For the most part, I have included Akao's interpolations from other manuscripts, apart from a few instances where they seemed repetitive, unrelated to or at variance with the text at hand. Although the original draft noted every major interpolation and every case in which the Fujimoto text was used in preference to the version in Akao, it was felt that such a format would be unnecessarily burdensome in a popular edition.

A word about the language of the sermons: Bankei's speaking style is simple and informal. He uses the everyday Japanese speech of his period, flavored at times with the dialect of his native province of Harima. Generally, he avoids technical Buddhist terms, except those readily familiar to his listeners, and his manner of expression tends to be relaxed and colloquial. It is important to remember that Bankei's sermons were spontaneous talks. As such, they have a direct, living quality that lends them their peculiar vigor and charm, but they are not "literature" and were never intended to be read. In placing the sermons into English, I sought to reproduce Bankei's distinctive tone and at the same time remain faithful to the original, aiming for a smooth translation of Bankei's words, but not trying to make them sound "better" than they are.

Ages are given as in the text. According to Japanese custom, one is considered a year old at birth, so that the age reckoned in Western terms is approximately one year less. Chinese names appear in their Japanese readings as Bankei would have pronounced them, as do all names from Indian sources. Only specialized Indian terms like "buddha" or "tathagata" are retained in the original.

SERMONS: PAGE REFERENCES TO ORIGINAL TEXTS

(Page references to the original texts employed in the translations follow each entry: BZZ *Bankei zenji zenshū*, BZK *Bankei zenji hōgoshū*.)

Opening of the sermons
(BZZ:3, BZH:3)

Listen carefully
(BZZ:3–6, BZH:4–5)

Precepts
(BZZ:6, BZH:205)

The same old thing
(BZZ:7, BZH:7)

I don't talk about Buddhism
(BZZ:8)

Meeting masters: Dōsha and In-gen
(BZZ:11–12, BZH:172)

I'm ready to be your witness!
(BZZ:12–18, BZH12–18, 175–190)

Growing up deluded
(BZZ:21–22, BZH:200–202)

Thirty days in the Unborn
(BZZ:22–23, BZH:29)

Ask me and I'll tell you
(BZZ:25)

"The Kappa"
(BZZ:28, BZH:36)

Don't beat sleeping monks
(BZZ:30–31, BZH:23–24)

Mind reading
(BZH:37)

Moving ahead/sliding back
(BZZ:31, BZH:37)

Old wastepaper
(BZZ:32, BZH:38)

Self-centeredness
(BZZ:32–33, BZH:38)

Bankei's Kannon
(BZZ:33)

Getting sidetracked
(BZZ:33–34, BZH:129–130)

Self-power/other-power
(BZZ:36)

Dreams
(BZZ:36)

Everybody has the Buddha Mind
(BZZ:37–42, BZH:47–56)

Being living buddhas
(BZZ:42–50, BZH:56–67)

Servants, samurai, husbands and wives
(BZZ:50–57, BZH:67–80)

"Buddha" Magoemon
(BZZ:61–62, BZH:81–83, 87)

Like little children of three or four
(BZZ:63–64, BZH:89–90)

Getting angry
(BZZ:64–65, BZH:90–92)

Blindness and the Unborn
(BZZ:65–66, BZH:92–93)

Now I'm going to talk to the women
(BZZ:70–71, BZH:102–105)

The old nurse from Sanuki
(BZZ:71–72)

Nothing to do with rules
(BZZ:34–35, BZH:106–107)

Devices
(BZZ:35, BZH:107)

Plain speaking
(BZZ:72–73, 28–29; BZH:107–109)

Illness and the Buddha Mind
(BZZ:73–74, BZH:109–111)

Being free in birth and death
  (BZZ:74–75, BZH:111–112)
The original face
  (BZZ:75–76)
Entrances
  (BZZ:76)
To practice is hard
  (BZZ:76–77)
The crow and the cormorant
  (BZZ:77)
Let it be
  (BZZ:77–78, BZH:116–117)
The lawsuit
  (BZZ:78–81, BZH:117–122)
Mu
  (BZZ:84–85)
The crows go kaa-kaa
  (BZZ:85)
Two-thirds is with the Unborn
  (BZZ:85–86, BZH:132)
Looking for enlightenment
  (BZZ:86)
No delusion, no enlightenment
  (BZZ:88, BZH:135)

Water and ice
  (BZZ:88–89, BZH:136–137)
Stopping thoughts
  (BZZ:89)
The mirror
  (BZZ:90, BZH:137–138)
Fire is hot
  (BZZ:90–91, BZH:138–139)
Be stupid!
  (BZZ:94–95)
Smoking
  (BZZ:95–96, BZH:139–140)
No such thing as enlightenment
  (BZZ:97–98, BZH:141–143)
Abide in the Buddha Mind
  (BZZ:98–99, BZH:143–144)
When thoughts arise
  (BZZ:99, BZH:144–145)
Letting things take care of themselves
  (BZZ:100–101, BZH:147–148)

HŌGO (Instruction)

The *Butchi Kōsai zenji hōgo* (*Dharma Instruction of the Zen Master Butchi Kōsai*) is a work in Japanese compiled in 1730 by Itsuzan Sonin (or Sojin, 1655–1734), one of Bankei's foremost disciples. Itsuzan became a monk at age ten, studying under a succession of Zen masters before coming to Bankei sometime around 1680. In 1683 he became Bankei's disciple and experienced enlightenment under him the following year. From 1688 till Bankei's death in 1693, Itsuzan was the closest of Bankei's personal attendants and in 1697 was made the Dharma heir of Bankei's successor Setsugai. In later life, he became abbot of the Nyohōji and served a term as abbot of the Myōshiuji, receiving the Imperial title of Shinshō Jōmyō Zenji ("Zen Master of True Nature Pure and Radiant").

Unlike the *Sermons*, the materials in the *Hōgo* are not verbatim records of Bankei's teachings but Itsuzan's recollections of various talks, dialogues and encounters, which he set down in old age as a kind of pious tribute to his late teacher. Because of Itsuzan's close connection with Bankei, the *Hōgo* provides a valuable first-hand account of the Master's teaching during the last decade or so of his career, and, though occasionally verging on hagiography, presents overall a lively and intimate picture of life in Bankei's assembly. The materials from the *Hōgo* are accompanied by several selections from the *Kōsai zenji gyōgō ryakki* (*Brief Account of the Activities of the Zen Master Kōsai*), a companion collection by Itsuzan.

"WORDS AND DEEDS"

During the eighteenth century, a number of accounts dealing with Bankei were compiled by priests in the teaching lines of the various temples he had founded. Ironically, despite Bankei's insistence on the importance of simple, ordinary Japanese language, these collections were composed entirely in literary Chinese and contain many technical Buddhist and Zen expressions. Aside from their complexity of style, it is often impossible to determine the accuracy of the information provided in these works, and it may be safest to consider them part of the "legend" of Bankei, a reflection of the way in which the Master came to be viewed in the period following his death.

The selections translated here are drawn primarily from two such collections: the *Shōgen kokushi itsujijō* (*Record of Anecdotes Concerning the National Teacher Shōgen**) by

---

*A posthumous title bestowed on Bankei by the Imperial Court in 1740.

Daitei Zenkei (d. 1788), a Zen Master in Bankei's teaching line; and the *Zeigo* ("*Redundant Words*") by Bankei's Dharma heir Sandō Chijō (d. 1749). Although it is doubtful that he ever studied with Bankei, Daitei was a member of the Nakabori family of Shimomura, grandson of the same Sukeyasu Nakabori who had enabled Bankei's father to establish himself in Hamada and had later assisted the young Bankei when his brother expelled him from the family home. As Daitei tells us, since childhood he had listened to stories about Bankei from his nursemaids and grandparents, and was thus in a unique position to preserve many of the homelier details of the Master's character and career. Sandō Chijō was twenty-six at the time of Bankei's death and eighty when he compiled the *Zeigo* in 1747. Sandō records certain interesting episodes not found elsewhere, but his account is marred by vituperative attacks on the other collections and what seems a dogmatic insistence on Bankei's place in the Myōshinji line, rejecting his enlightenment under Dōsha and stressing his debt to Umpo.

Other works represented in this section are the *Tomisusanshi*, an extensive collection of materials relating to Bankei and the Nyohōji recorded by the temple's abbot Gottan Sobi (n.d.) in 1798; and the *Ryōmonji shiryaku*, a history of the Ryōmonji compiled in 1700 by Bankei's disciple Genmon Eigin (d. 1747), a nephew of Bankei's friend and patron Sasaki Nobutsugu.